Autodesk AutoCAD Mechanical Drafting For Beginners

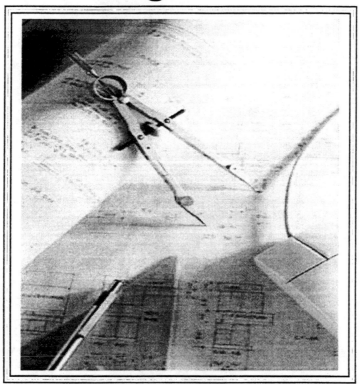

Elise Moss

authorized author

SDC
PUBLICATIONS

Schroff Development Corporation
www.SDCACAD.com

Schroff Development Corporation
P.O. Box 1334
Mission, KS 66222
(913) 262-2664
www.schroff.com

Moss, Elise
      Autodesk AutoCAD2000i Mechanical Drafting for
Beginners/
      Elise Moss
ISBN: 1-58503-068-6

The author and publisher of this book have used their best efforts in preparing this book.
These efforts include the development, research, and testing of material presented. The
author and publisher shall not be held liable in any event for incidental or consequential
damages with, or arising out of, the furnishing, performance, or use of the material
herein.

Printed and bound in the United States of America.

Preface

This book began as a series of class notes and power points during my tenure at Silicon Valley College. The material was expanded and grew for my classes at DeAnza Community College. When Schroff Development Corporation approached me to write this textbook, I was initially reluctant. After all, there are a plethora of textbooks on the market for AutoCAD and I didn't feel that I had anything additional I could add.

I was convinced to go forward with this text because the class notes I prepared for my classes would often go through double and even triple printings at the DeAnza College Bookstore. This meant that people who were not even enrolled in my class were coming into the bookstore to purchase my notes. Obviously, my material was filling in gaps.

The major gap was applying the knowledge of AutoCAD to mechanical drafting. Knowing how to draw a line in AutoCAD is not the same as understanding which line type is required when creating technical drawings. This text provides the necessary information on how to use AutoCAD as a tool to work as a mechanical drafter or designer.

This text should be used to in combination with a basic AutoCAD reference manual or with an instructor who can provide guidance on basic AutoCAD.

The PowerPoints used in this text can be downloaded from www.schroff.com.

Acknowledgements

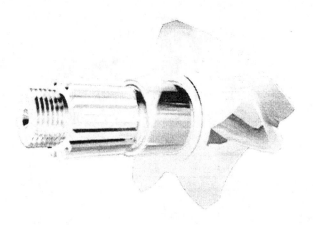

This book would not have been possible without the support of some key Autodesk employees. A special thanks to Susie Chang, Derrick Smith, Alan Jacobs, Rebecca Bell, Lynn Allen, Melrose Ross, Denis Cadu, Carolyn Gavriloff, and David Koel.

Additional thanks to the board and members of the Silicon Valley AutoCAD Power Users, a dedicated group of Autodesk users, for educating me about the needs and wants of CAD users.

The effort and support of the editorial and production staff of Schroff Development Corporation is gratefully acknowledged. I especially thank Stephen Schroff for his helpful suggestions regarding the format of this text.

Finally, truly infinite thanks to Ari for his encouragement and his faith.

Elise Moss
Los Gatos, CA

Table of Contents

Table of Contents

Introduction

AutoCAD introduced Model vs. Paper Space in Release 10. The idea was that mechanical engineers would create a 3D model in model space and then place the various views (front, right side, top, isometric) in paper space. Instead, most mechanical engineers tried manipulating paper vs. model space and decided that since most of the drafting at the time was 2D, they would just stay in model space and ignore paper space. Architects love paper space because they can draw their floor plans and elevations 1:1 and then use paper space to scale their views.

Some mechanical engineers will create their 2D detail drawing in model space and then create one large viewport in layout. They will insert their title block and dimensions in paper space (layout).

For the purposes of this text, all drafting is done in model space. This textbook only deals with 2D mechanical drafting and the only reason to use paper space is to utilize viewports.

I expect that as more companies move into the 3D world, they will utilize software programs such as Mechanical Desktop and Inventor. But this will not eliminate the need to know AutoCAD. There is almost twenty years of legacy data out there, all drawn in 2D. Those drawings will need to be maintained. Additionally, sheet metal and machine shops will continue to require 2D drawings in order to fabricate parts.

Lesson 1
Navigating AutoCAD's Coordinate System

Learning Objectives:

- The UCS Icon
- Direct Entry
- Absolute Coordinates
- Relative Coordinates
- Polar Coordinates

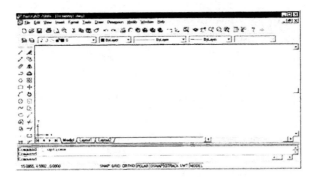

When you first start AutoCAD, you see a menu, a command line, several toolbars, and a graphics window. The graphics window is divided into Model Space and Paper Space/Layout.

The graphics window uses a Cartesian coordinate system. The lower left corner of the screen shows a UCS (user coordinate system) icon. The icon shows x for horizontal and y for vertical. The UCS is located at the 0,0 or origin point.

```
Command: _.options
Command:
Command:

 11.4975, 2.2944 , 0.0000              SNAP GRID
```

At the lower left corner of your screen, you will see some numbers. These numbers reflect the coordinate point (x,y) of your mouse. Move your mouse around and note how the coordinate values change.

TIP: Use F6 to toggle your coordinates ON and off.

Your graphics window in AutoCAD emulates a piece of paper. LIMITS controls the size of your piece of paper. When you start a new file, you can specify the size of paper you want to draw on using Wizard or Templates. AutoCAD really doesn't care where you draw in your graphics window. You can draw outside the limits with impunity.

AutoCAD allows you to draw geometry using four methods:

- Absolute Coordinates
- Relative Coordinates
- Polar Coordinates
- Direct Entry

Absolute Coordinates use absolute values relative to the origin.

Relative Coordinates use coordinates relative to the last point selected.

Polar Coordinates use a distance and angle relative to the last point selected.

Direct Entry allows the user to set ORTHO on (this is like using a ruler to draw a straight line), move the mouse in the desired direction, and then enter in the desired distance.

Exercise 1: Absolute Coordinates

Draw the figure shown by entering in the absolute coordinates.

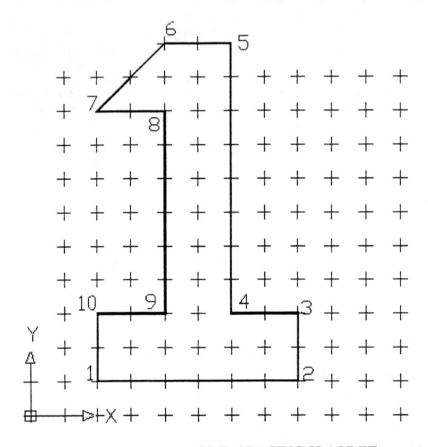

GRID SPACING IS 1 UNIT

1. START POINT IS 2,1	6. 4, 11
2. 8,1	7. 2, 9
3. 8,3	8. 4, 9
4. 6,3	9. 4, 3
5. 6, 11	10. 2, 3

TIP: Use GRID and SNAP to assist you in drawing the figure. Use CLOSE to close your figure.

Exercise 2: Relative Coordinates

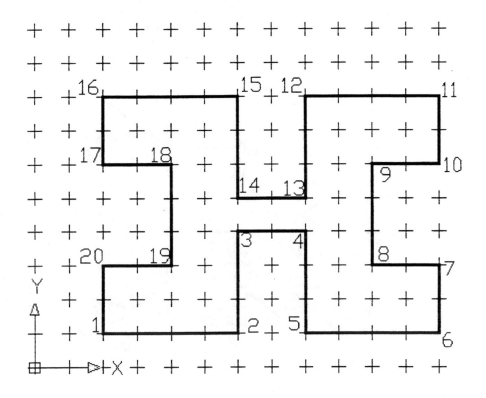

1 UNIT SPACE

1. START AT 2,1	11.
2. @4,0	12.
3. @0, 3	13.
4. @2,0	14.
5. @0, -3	15.
6. @4, 0	16
7. @0, 2	17.
8. @-2, 0	18.
9. @0, 3	19.
10. @2,0	20.

FILL IN THE COORDINATES BEFORE STARTING THE DRAWING.

Exercise 3: Polar Coordinates

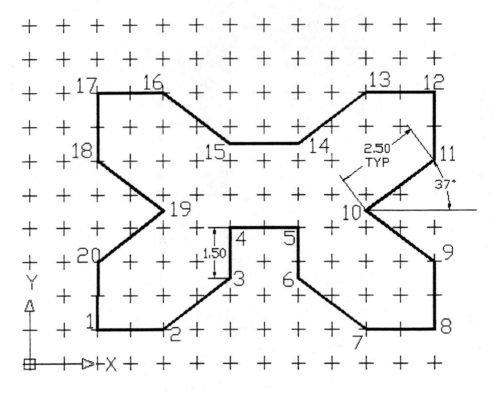

1 UNIT SPACE

FORMAT IS DISTANCE < ANGLE
REFERENCE POINT IS THE LAST POINT ENTERED

START POINT 2,1	11.
2. @2<0	12.
3. @2.5<37	13.
4. @1.5<90	14.
5. @2<0	15.
6. @2<-270	16.
7. @2.5<-37	17.
8. @2<0	18.
9. @2<90	19.
10. @-2.5<-37	20.

FILL IN THE COORDINATES BEFORE STARTING THE DRAWING.

Exercise 4: Mixed Coordinates

Draw an object by connecting the point coordinates below.

Points	Coordinates	Points	Coordinates
1	2,2	8	@-1.5,0
2	@1.5,0	9	@0,1.25
3	@.75<90	10	@-1.25,1.25
4	@1.5<0	11	@2<180
5	@0,-.75	12	@-1.25,-1.25
6	@3,0	13	@2.25<270
7	@1<90		

Exercise 5: Direct Entry

Direct entry requires that you enable ORTHO mode.

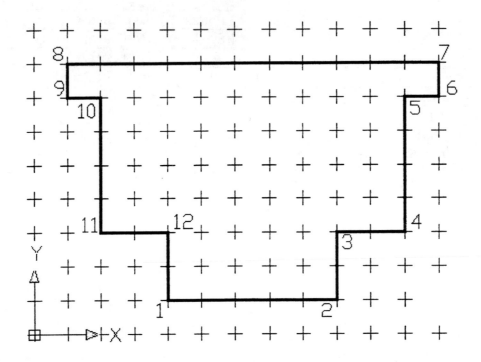

1 UNIT SPACING

1. START AT 4, 1	7.
2. MOUSE RIGHT 5 UNITS	8.
3. MOUSE UP 2 UNITS	9.
4. MOUSE RIGHT 2 UNITS	10.
5. MOUSE UP 4 UNITS	11.
6. MOUSE RIGHT 1 UNIT	12.

FILL IN THE COORDINATES BEFORE STARTING THE DRAWING.

TIP: Use F8 to toggle ORTHO ON or OFF or use the ORTHO button on the bottom of the screen.

Lesson 2
Polylines

Learning Objectives:

- Polyline
- Polyline edit

Primarily, GIS drafters and architects use polylines. Mechanical drafters use polylines to create drawing borders, arrows and cutting plane lines. Cutting plane lines are used for section views.

A polyline is similar to a line but it can have thickness. Additionally, you can "join" or connect more than one line to create a single object. Polylines can have varying thickness or widths.

Polylines can be created four ways:

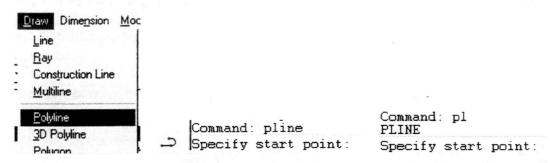

Menu	Draw-> Polyline
Draw Toolbar	⤵
Command line:	pline
Shortcut	pl

The polyline command has several options:
```
[Arc/Halfwidth/Length/Undo/Width]:
```

Arc	Creates Polyarc
Halfwidth	Specifies half the width of the polyline
Length	Specifies the length of the polyline segment
Undo	Undoes the last point selected
Width	Specifies the width of the polyline

You can draw your object using lines and arcs and convert it to polyline using the polyline edit command. You can convert polylines and polyarcs back to lines and arcs using the EXPLODE command.

TIP: The PLINEGEN system variable controls the linetype pattern display around and the smoothness of the vertices of a 2D polyline. Setting PLINEGEN to 1 generates new polylines in a continuous pattern around the vertices of the completed polyline. Setting PLINEGEN to 0 starts and ends the polyline with a dash at each vertex. PLINEGEN does not apply to polylines with tapered segments. This is a new feature in AutoCAD2000i.

PLINETYPE controls both the creation of new polylines with the PLINE command and the conversion of existing polylines in drawings from previous releases.

0 Polylines in older drawings are not converted when opened; PLINE creates old-format polylines

1 Polylines in older drawings are not converted when opened; PLINE creates optimized polylines

2 Polylines in older drawings are converted when opened; PLINE creates optimized polylines

The CONVERT command can be used to optimize polylines created in AutoCAD R13 or earlier.

Sometimes it is easier for the beginner drafter to create the geometry using standard lines and arcs and then convert the geometry into polylines and polyarcs. To change a regular line to a polyline, use the PEDIT command. PEDIT can also be used to modify the width to an existing polylines and append geometry.

The polyline edit command can be initiated four ways:

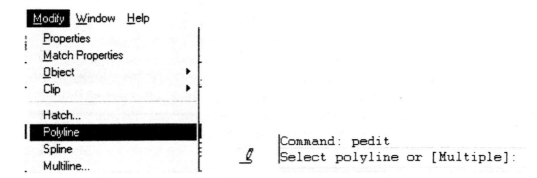

```
Command: pedit
Select polyline or [Multiple]:
```

```
Command: pe
PEDIT Select polyline or [Multiple]:
```

Menu	Modify-> Polyline
Modify II Toolbar	
Command line:	pedit
Shortcut	pe

The PEDIT command has several options:

```
[Close/Join/Width/Edit vertex/Fit/Spline/Decurve/Ltype gen/Undo]:
```

Close	Creates the closing segment of the polyline, connecting the last segment with the first. AutoCAD considers the polyline open unless you close it using the Close option.
Open	Removes the closing segment of the polyline. AutoCAD considers the polyline closed unless you open it using the Open option.
Join	Adds lines, arcs, or polylines to the end of an open polyline and removes the curve fitting from a curve-fit polyline. For objects to join the polyline, their endpoints must touch unless you use the Multiple option at the first PEDIT prompt. In this case, you can join polylines that do not touch if the fuzz distance is set to a value large enough to include the endpoints.
Width	Specifies a new uniform width for the entire polyline.
Edit Vertex	Marks the first vertex of the polyline by drawing an X on the screen. If you have specified a tangent direction for this vertex, an arrow is also drawn in that direction.
Fit	Creates a smooth curve consisting of pairs of arcs joining each pair of vertices. The curve passes through all vertices of the polyline and uses any tangent direction you specify.
Spline	Uses the vertices of the selected polyline as the control points, or frame, of a curve. The curve passes through the first and last control points unless the original polyline was closed. The curve is pulled toward the other points but does not necessarily pass through them. The more control points you specify in a particular part of the frame, the more pull they exert on the curve. The technical term for this type of curve is *B-spline*. AutoCAD can generate quadratic and cubic spline-fit polylines.
Decurve	Removes extra vertices inserted by a fit or spline curve and straightens all segments of the polyline. Retains tangent information assigned to the polyline vertices for use in subsequent fit curve requests. If you edit a spline-fit polyline with commands such as BREAK or TRIM, you cannot use the Decurve option.
Ltype gen	Generates the linetype in a continuous pattern through the vertices of the polyline. When turned off, this option generates the linetype starting and ending with a dash at each vertex. Ltype Gen does not apply to polylines with tapered segments.
Undo	Reverses operations as far back as the beginning of the PEDIT session.

Exercise 1: Drawing an arrow

Polylines are very handy for creating an arrow shape.

```
Command: _pline
Specify start point: 2,2

Current line-width is 0.0000
Specify next point or [Arc/Halfwidth/Length/Undo/Width]: w

Specify starting width <0.0000>:  <ENTER>

Specify ending width <0.0000>: 0.8

Specify next point or [Arc/Halfwidth/Length/Undo/Width]:  <Ortho on> .75

Specify next point or [Arc/Close/Halfwidth/Length/Undo/Width]: w

Specify starting width <0.8000>: 0.04

Specify ending width <0.0400>:  <ENTER>

Specify next point or [Arc/Close/Halfwidth/Length/Undo/Width]: 5

Specify next point or [Arc/Close/Halfwidth/Length/Undo/Width]:  <ENTER>
```

Exercise 2:

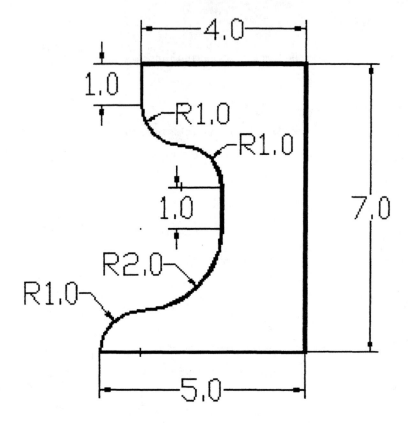

Draw the figure shown using polylines and polyarcs with a width of 0.04.

Exercise 3:

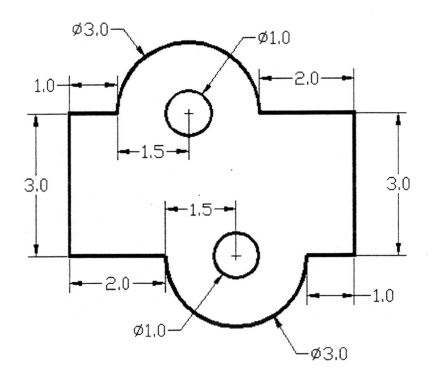

Use donut with W = 0.05 to create the circles.
Use polyline and polyarc with width = 0.04 to draw the outside figure.

Exercise 4:

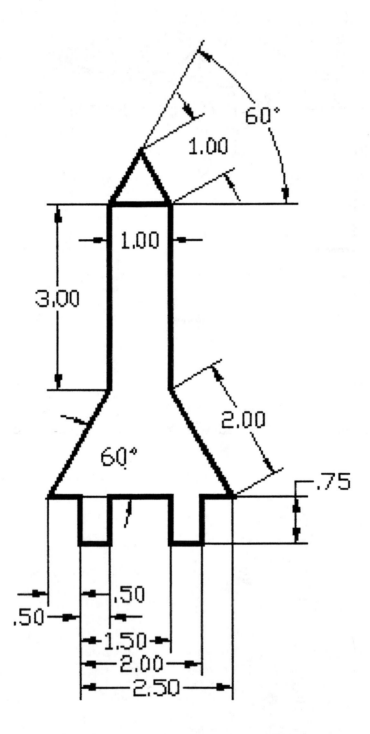

Drawing using polyline with a width of 0.04.

Lesson 3

Linetypes and Layers

Learning Objectives

- Loading linetypes
- Using linetypes
- Setting up layers
- Creating layer standards

COMMON LINETYPES

- OBJECT LINES
  - HIDDEN LINES
    - CENTER LINES
      - EXTENSION LINES
        - DIMENSION LINES
          - LEADER LINES
            - PHANTOM LINES

OBJECT LINES

ALSO CALLED VISIBLE LINES

SHOW THE OUTLINE OF AN OBJECT

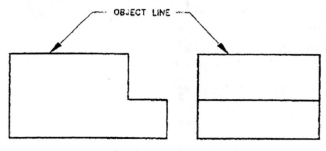

Fig. 6-2. Object line.

USE CONTINUOUS LINETYPE

HIDDEN LINES

OFTEN CALLED

DASHED LINES

USED TO
REPRESENT THE
INVISIBLE EDGES
OF AN OBJECT

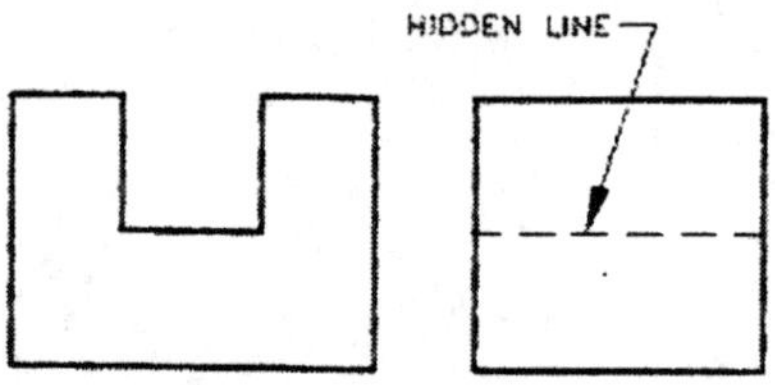

Fig. 6-3. Hidden line.

USE HIDDEN LINETYPE

CENTER LINES

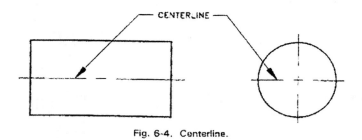

Fig. 6-4. Centerline.

LOCATE THE CENTERS OF CIRCLES & ARCS

USE CENTER LINETYPE

EXENSION LINES

SHOW THE EXTENT OF A
DIMENSION.

BEGIN A SMALL
DISTANCE AWAY FROM
THE OBJECT & EXTEND.

MAY CROSS OBJECT
LINES, HIDDEN LINES,
AND CENTER LINES.

MAY NOT CROSS OTHER
EXTENSION LINES.

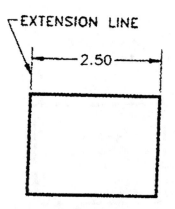

Fig. 6-5. Extension line.

USE DIM, LINEAR TO CREATE

DIMENSION LINES

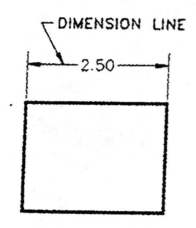

Fig. 6-6. Dimension line.

PLACED BETWEEN
EXTENSION LINES.

BROKEN NEAR THE
CENTER TO ALLOW
PLACEMENT OF
NUMERALS.

ARROWS ON EACH
END.

LEADER LINES

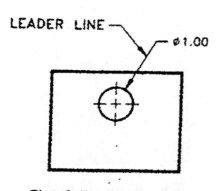

Fig. 6-7. Leader line.

USED TO CONNECT A
SPECIFIC NOTE TO A
FEATURE.

SHOULD BE AT A 45
DEGREE ANGLE

STARTS WITH AN
ARROW AND HAS A
SMALL SHOULDER
AT THE NOTE

USE DIM, LEADER

PHANTOM LINES

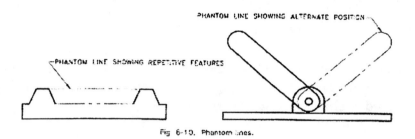

Fig 6-10. Phantom lines.

USED TO SHOW REPETITIVE FEATURES

USED TO SHOW MOTION

USED TO SHOW ALTERNATE
PART/PLACEMENT

USE PHANTOM LINETYPE

When you start AutoCAD, the only linetype available is CONTINUOUS. This is the linetype used primarily for object lines. In order to keep file sizes small, the user must load any other desired linetype before he can draw using that line style.

TIP: Once you load a linetype it remains in the drawing's database even if you don't have any geometry with that linetype. To keep your file size small, you should routinely run the PURGE command to eliminate unused linetypes and layers.

To load a linetype, the user has several options:

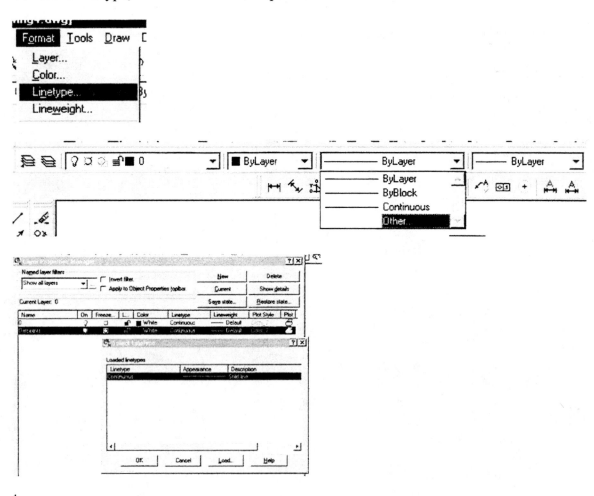

```
Command: linetype
```

```
Command: lt
```

Menu	Format->Linetype
Object Properties Toolbar	Select Other on the Linetype dropdown
Layer Properties Manager Dialog	Left pick on the linetype column
Command line:	Linetype
Shortcut	LT

Any of these methods will bring up the Linetype Manager.

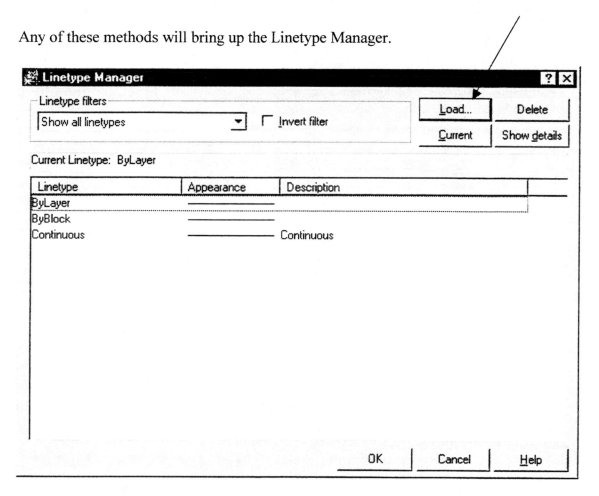

To load additional linetypes, press the Load button.

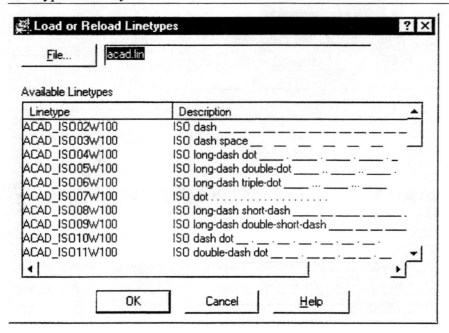

The Load or Reload Linetypes dialog box appears. The user can select one or more linetypes to load and press 'OK'.

TIP: To select more than one linetype to load at a time, hold down the CONTROL key.

Exercise 1: Loading Linetypes

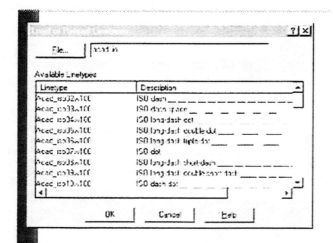

SELECT THE
FOLLOWING
LINETYPES:

HIDDEN

CENTER

PHANTOM

SELECT BY HIGHLIGHTING WITH
MOUSE.

PRESS

'OK'.

HOLD DOWN CTL KEY FOR MULTIPLE
SELECTIONS.

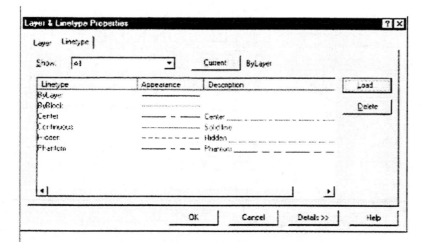

PRESS

'OK'.

SELECTED LINETYPES SHOULD BE
DISPLAYED IN THE PROPERTIES WINDOW.

The architectural industry has set up layer standards defining colors and linetypes to be used when creating drawings. The mechanical engineering industry has not developed a standard to be used for layers. Each company usually creates their own standards to be used for all technical documents. This ensures that the drawings have a uniform appearance.

TIP: One method to ensure that all drafters comply with a company's standards is to use a template set up with layers and linetypes. Use of templates is discussed later in this text.

Layers are used to organize your drawing. Industry standard is to place object lines, hidden, dimensions, etc. each on a separate layer. Many drafters organize their drawings by placing object types on separate layers. For example, fasteners, doors, walls, gears might each be placed on a separate layer. Layer names should be short but easy to understand.

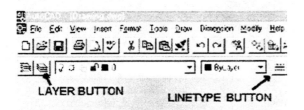

YOU CAN USE THE LAYER CONTROL & LINETYPE CONTROL TO SET UP YOUR LAYERS TO USE THE DIFFERENT LINETYPES

START BY CLICKING ON THE LAYER BUTTON

Exercise 2: Creating Layers

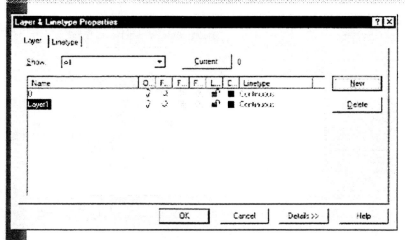

CLICK ON

THE 'NEW'
BUTTON.

THE NEW
LAYER IS
HIGHLIGHTED.

RENAME THE NEW LAYER 'OBJECT'

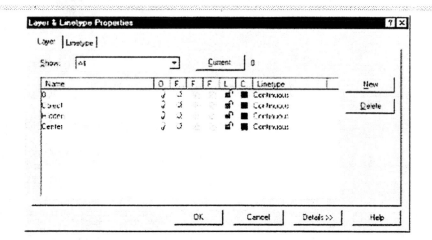

ADD LAYERS FOR HIDDEN AND CENTER LINES.

TIP: You can create more than one layer at a time by typing a comma at the end of your layer name.

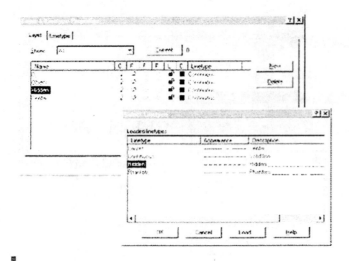

HIGHLIGHT THE
LAYER CALLED
'HIDDEN'.

CLICK ON THE
WORD
'CONTINUOUS'.

HIGHLIGHT THE
LINETYPE
'HIDDEN'.

PRESS

'OK'.

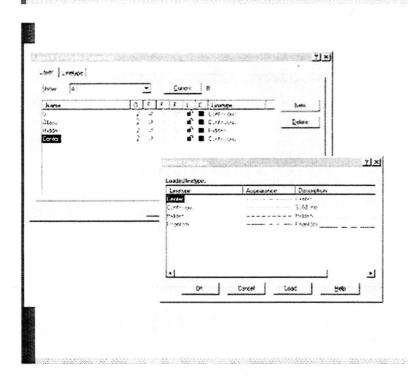

HIGHLIGHT THE
LAYER NAMED
'CENTER'.

CLICK ON THE
LINETYPE.

SELECT
'CENTER'.

PRESS

'OK' TWICE.

Set the layers so that they use the following color scheme:

Object	Green
Hidden	Cyan
Phantom	Red

TO SET WHICH LAYER IS
CURRENT, HIGHLIGHT THE
LAYER AND CLICK
CURRENT BUTTON.

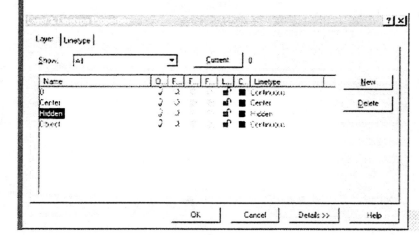

PRESS

'OK'.

Exercise 3:

TRY SWITCHING LAYERS

DRAW A LINE TO SEE
WHAT IT LOOKS LIKE.

SWITCH AGAIN.

QUIZ

1.　　The coordinate @ 2 < 45 is this type of coordinate:

　　　A. absolute
　　　B. relative
　　　C. polar
　　　D. positive

2.　　Which toolbar contains the Layer Control drop-down list?

　　　A. Draw
　　　B. Modify II
　　　C. Standard
　　　D. Object Properties

3.　　You need to create a number of layers in the current drawing file. From the following list, the name not considered a valid layer name is:

　　　A. 1
　　　B. $MECHANICAL
　　　C. FIRST FLOOR
　　　D. WIREFRAME_1

4.　　Which operation can not be performed using the Layer Control drop-down list?

　　　A. Change the color of a layer
　　　B. Freeze a layer
　　　C. Unlock a layer
　　　D. Turn on a layer

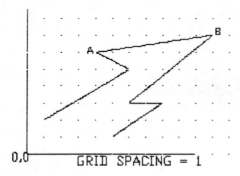

GRID SPACING = 1

5.   The relative coordinate from Point B to Point A is:

   A. @-7,1
   B. @1, 7
   C. @-7,-1
   D. @7,-1

6.   To turn the coordinate display located on the lower left corner of your screen on/off, use:

   A. F3
   B. F4
   C. F5
   D. F6

7.   Which of the following is NOT a valid coordinate entry?

   A. 2.5,9
   B. @4.185>18
   C. @1'3-1/2,11
   D. @8<90

8.   The coordinate @2,2 is this type of coordinate:

   A.   absolute
   B.   relative
   C.   polar
   D.   positive

T F 9.   Thawing a layer will cause water to condense on your monitor.
T F 10.   Absolute coordinates are relative to the last given point.

11. Name the three most common linetypes used in drafting.

    A.   HIDDEN, CONTINUOUS, DASHED
    B.   PHANTOM, HIDDEN, CENTER
    C.   CONTINUOUS, CENTER, HIDDEN
    D.   DASHED, PHANTOM, DOTTED

12.   The linetype used for objects is:

    A.   HIDDEN
    B.   DASHED
    C.   CENTER
    D.   CONTINUOUS

13.   The coordinate 2,2 is this type of coordinate:

    A.   absolute
    B.   relative
    C.   polar
    D.   positive

14.   You enter a coordinate value of @4<180. The @ symbol means:

    A.   relative to 0,0
    B.   relative to origin
    C.   relative to the last point entered
    D.   relative to the next point entered

T F 15.   An unused layer or linetype can never be deleted once you add them to the drawing.

16.   To add more than one layer at a time, type ___ at the end of each layer name.

    A.   :
    B.   ;
    C.   ,
    D.   "

17. These coordinates are located with repect to 0,0.

    A. POLAR
    B. RELATIVE
    C. CARTESIAN
    D. ABSOLUTE

T F 18.   The three types of Cartesian coordinates are Absolute, Relative, and Polar.
T F 19.   Layers are sorted alphabetically in the layer dialog box.
T F 20.   Freezing a layer can cause your system to freeze up.

21.   The coordinates displayed in the lower left corner of your screen are _____.

    A. absolute
    B. relative to the last point entered
    C. related to the limits
    D. Irrelevant

1) C; 2) D; 3) C; 4) A; 5) C; 6) D; 7) B; 8) B; 9) F; 10) F; 11) C; 12) D; 13) A; 14) C; 15) F; 16) C; 17) D; 18) T; 19) T; 20) F; 21) A

Lesson 4
Orthographic Views

Learning Objectives:

- How to layout a mechanical drawing
- How to select a Front View

FIRST-ANGLE PROJECTION

The U.S. and Canada uses Third-Angle Projection.

The rest of the world uses first-angle projection.

All countries start with a FRONT VIEW.

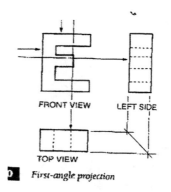

First-angle projection

THIRD- ANGLE PROJECTION

THIS IS THE LAYOUT USED IN THE UNITED STATES & CANADA.

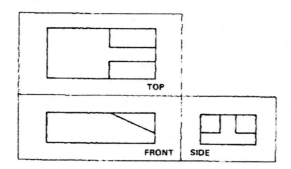

SELECTING A FRONT VIEW

THE CRITICAL PART OF LAYING OUT YOUR
DRAWING IS SELECTING YOUR FRONT VIEW.

- MINIMAL HIDDEN LINES

- STABLE - SO HEAVIEST PART IS ON BOTTOM

- USE THE MOST BASIC PROFILE

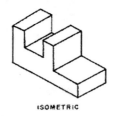

ISOMETRIC

COMMON ERROR # 1

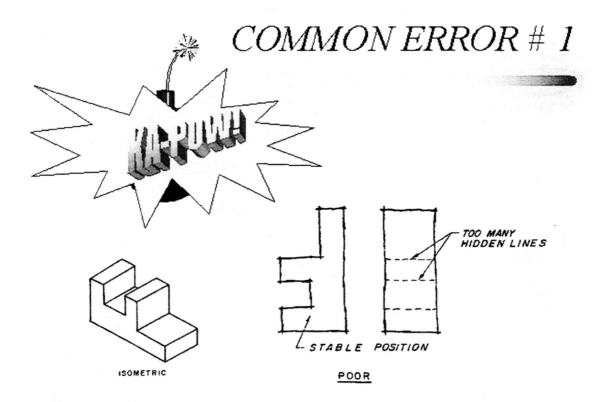

ISOMETRIC

STABLE POSITION

POOR

TOO MANY
HIDDEN LINES

COMMON ERROR #2

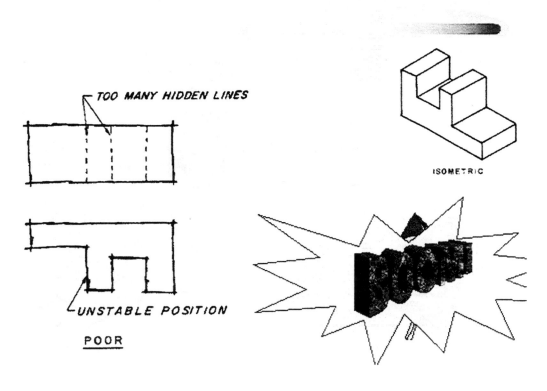

TOO MANY HIDDEN LINES

ISOMETRIC

UNSTABLE POSITION

POOR

COMMON ERROR #3

DON'T BE BEHIND THE EIGHT BALL!

NOT PROFILE

ISOMETRIC

POOR CHOICE   POOR CHOICE

COMMON ERROR #4

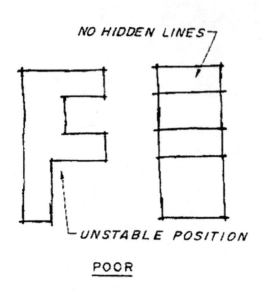

NO HIDDEN LINES

UNSTABLE POSITION

POOR

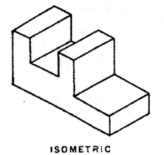

ISOMETRIC

THE CORRECT CHOICE!!!

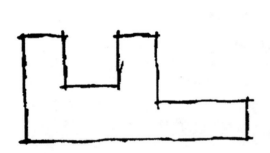

GOOD CHOICE-GOOD POSITION

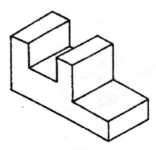

ISOMETRIC

LAYOUT EXAMPLE

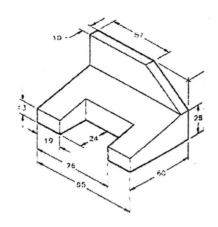

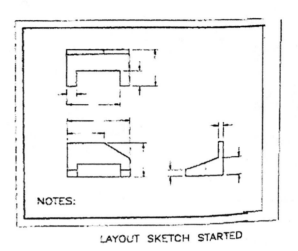

NOTES:

LAYOUT SKETCH STARTED

ORTHO LAYOUT WORKSHEET

SELECT THE CORRECT LAYOUT FOR THE THREE ISOMETRIC OBJECTS

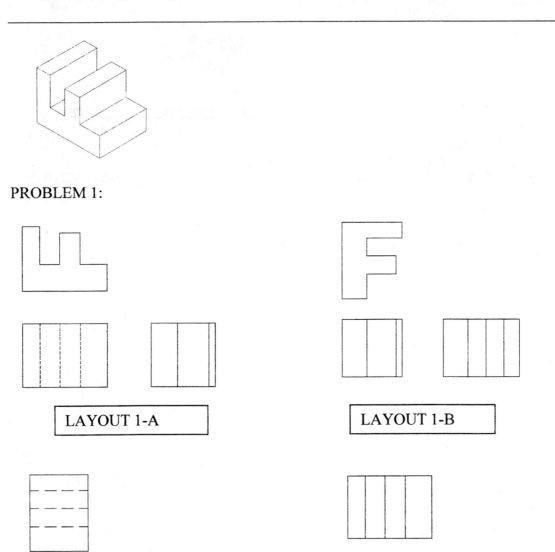

PROBLEM 1:

LAYOUT 1-A

LAYOUT 1-B

LAYOUT 1-C

LAYOUT 1-D

PROBLEM 2:

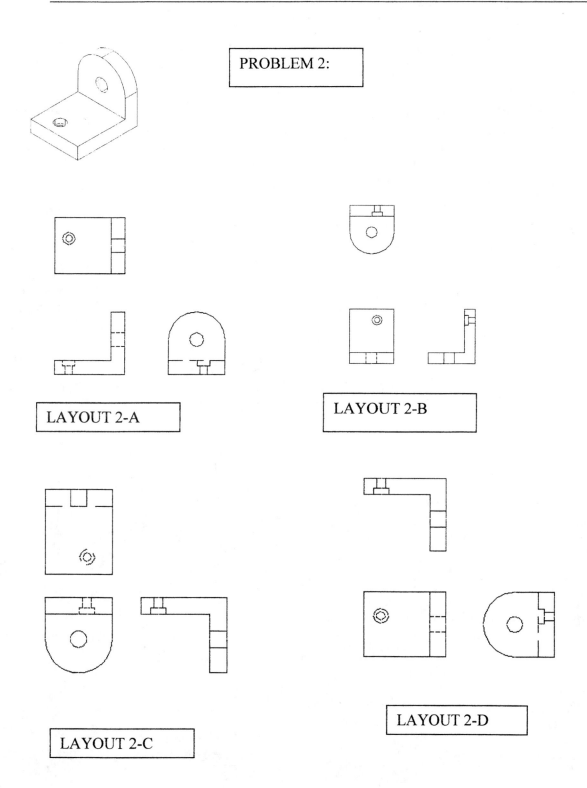

LAYOUT 2-A

LAYOUT 2-B

LAYOUT 2-C

LAYOUT 2-D

PROBLEM 3:

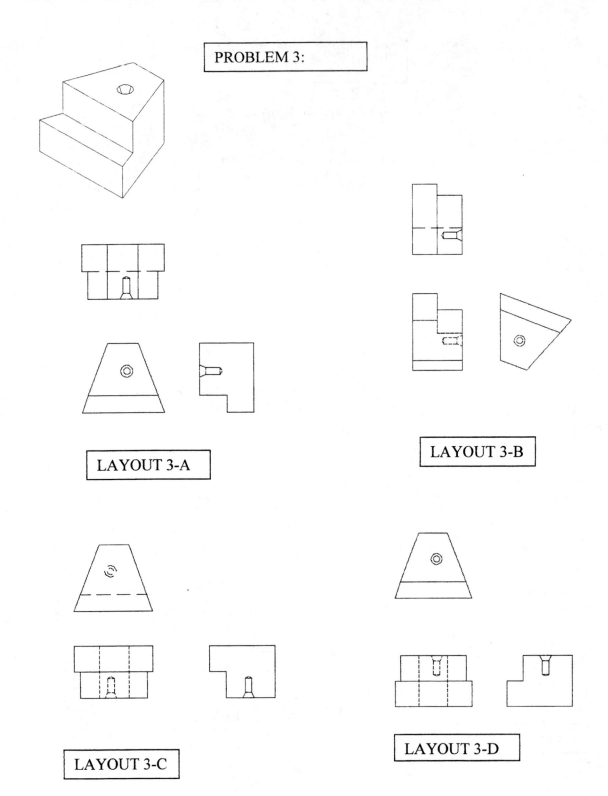

LAYOUT 3-A

LAYOUT 3-B

LAYOUT 3-C

LAYOUT 3-D

Lesson 5
Dimensioning

Learning Objectives:

- ANSI Dimensioning Standards
- Controlling Dimension Styles

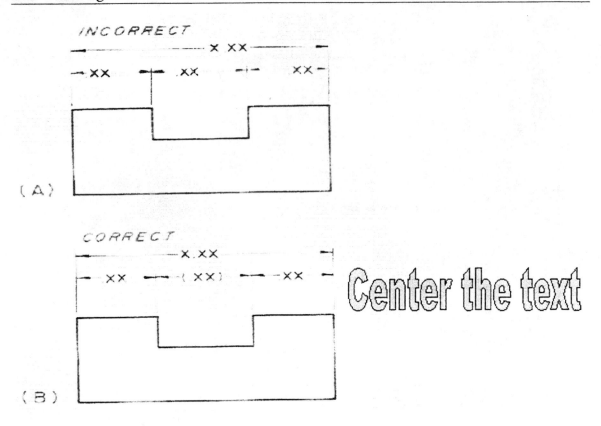

You can control the text placement by using the Dimension Text Edit tool on the Dimension toolbar.

You can also use GRIPS to move dimension text.

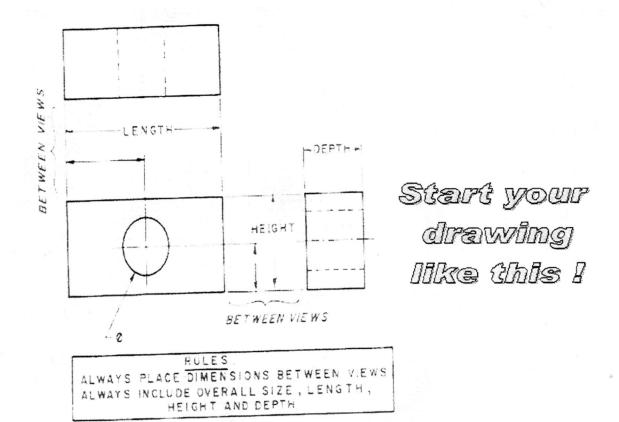

RULES
ALWAYS PLACE DIMENSIONS BETWEEN VIEWS
ALWAYS INCLUDE OVERALL SIZE , LENGTH ,
HEIGHT AND DEPTH

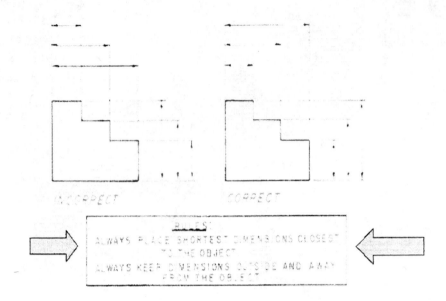

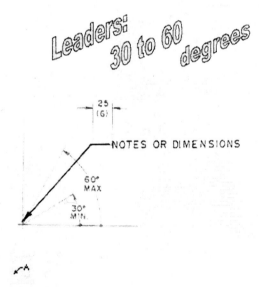

Use Baseline Dimensioning to place dimensions.

You can use the Settings tool within Leader to control how the leaders are placed.

```
Command: _qleader
Specify first leader point, or [Settings] <Settings>:
```

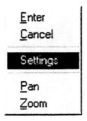

When you initiate the QLEADER command, one of the options is SETTINGS.
To enter this option, right click to select Settings or type S at the command line.

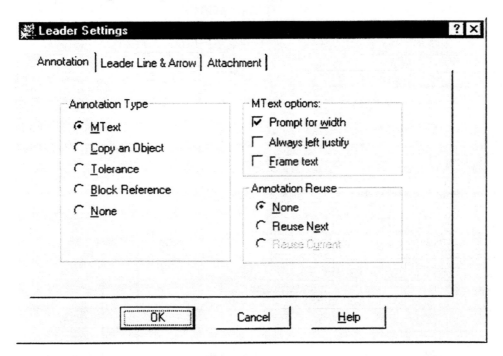

The Leader Settings dialog box appears.

Select the Leader Line & Arrow tab.

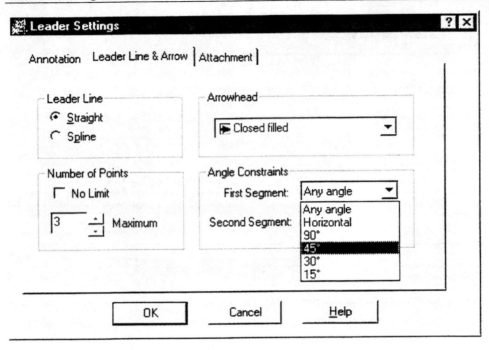

Set the First Segment to 45 degrees under Angle Constraints.

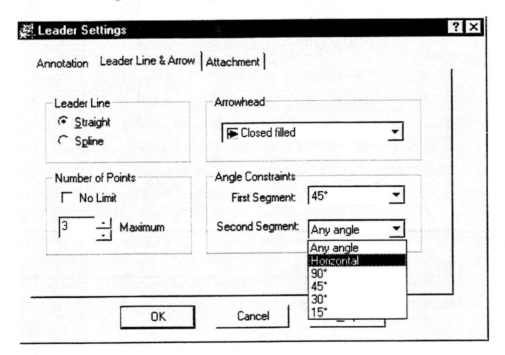

Set the Second Segment to Horizontal under Angle Constraints.

Press 'OK'.

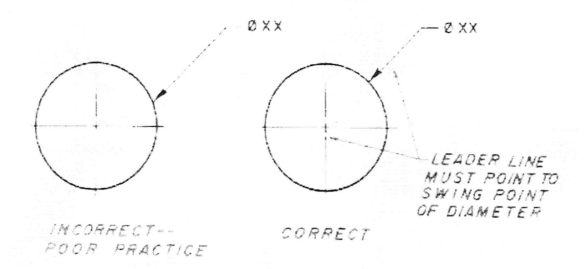

AutoCAD automatically sets diameter and radial dimensions to point to the swing point of the diameter. However, if you use GRIPS to move your dimension you may cause it to misalign. Use GRIPS with care.

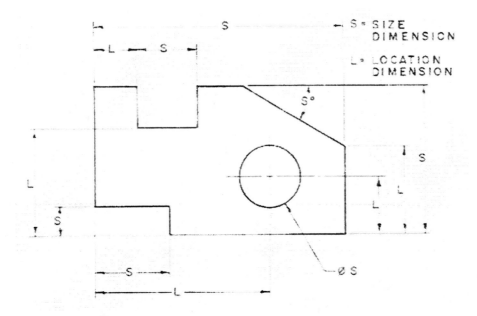

An example of how to properly dimension a view.

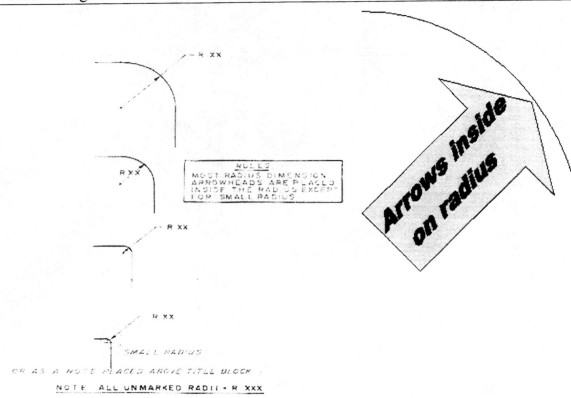

RULES
MOST RADIUS DIMENSION
ARROWHEADS ARE PLACED
INSIDE THE RADIUS EXCEPT
FOR SMALL RADIUS

R XX

R XX

R XX

R XX

SMALL RADIUS

OR AS A NOTE PLACED ABOVE TITLE BLOCK

NOTE ALL UNMARKED RADII - R XXX

Arrows inside on radius

To set your dimensions so that your arrows are placed inside the radius, you need to modify your Dimension Style.

The Dimension Style Manager may be accessed by:

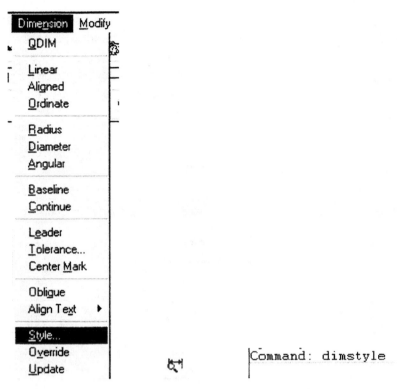

Command: dimstyle

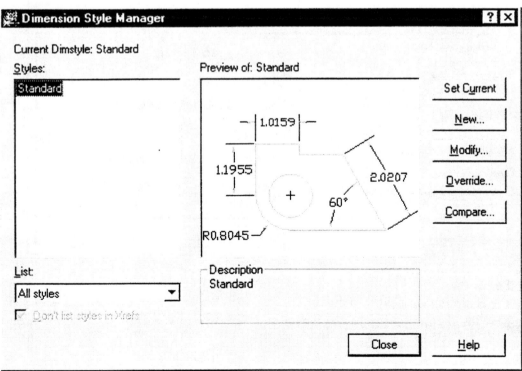

The Dimension Style Manager has a graphics window that preview changes made to the current style.

Architects will often create many different styles to manage the requirements of different counties and cities. Most mechanical drafters will create one style for standard (inch) dimensioning and one style for metric. Dimensioning styles for mechanical drawings are dictated by the American Society of Mechanical Engineers (ASME). A copy of the standards can be purchased through the ASME website at www.asme.org. The current dimensioning standards are ASME Y14.5M-1994. Most jobs require drafters to be familiar with ANSI dimensioning standards.

To modify the current dimension style, press the Modify button.

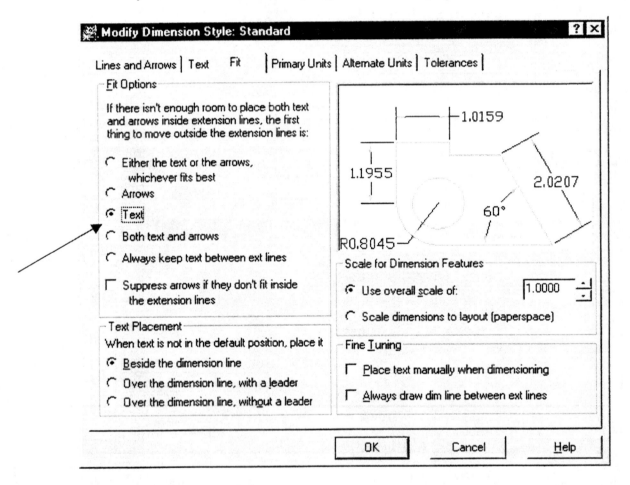

Select the Fit tab.
Enable the radio button next to the word Text.
Notice how the radial dimension changes in preview window.

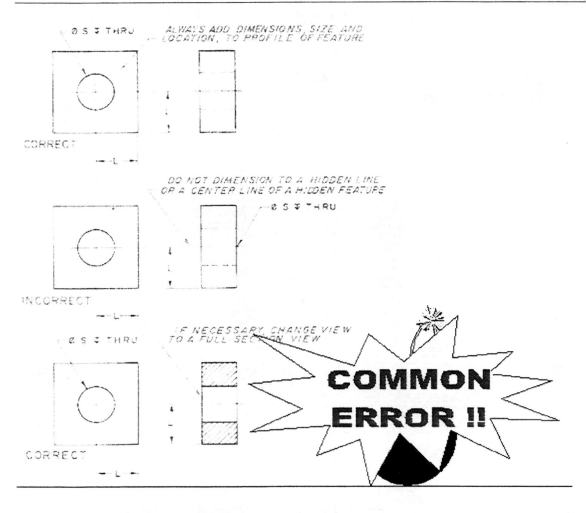

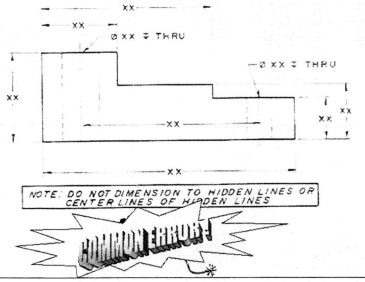

NOTE: DO NOT DIMENSION TO HIDDEN LINES OR CENTER LINES OF HIDDEN LINES

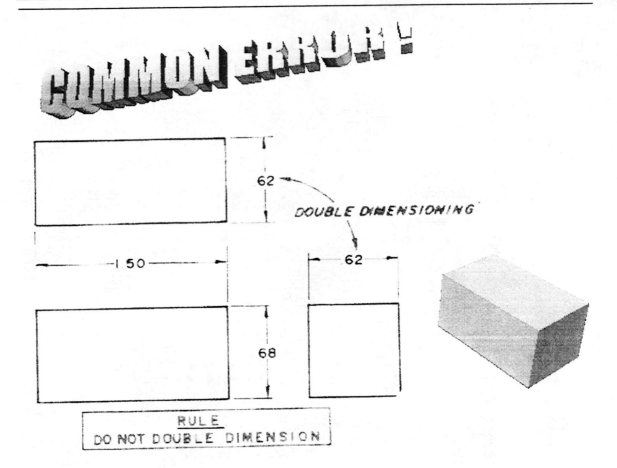

DOUBLE DIMENSIONING

62

1.50

62

68

RULE
DO NOT DOUBLE DIMENSION

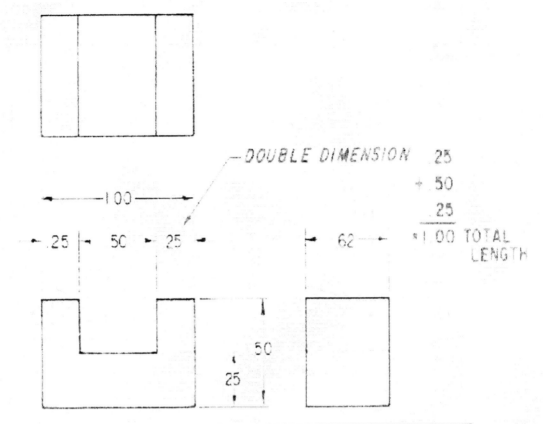

DOUBLE DIMENSION

.25
+ .50
.25

*1.00 TOTAL LENGTH

|—100—|

|— .25 —| |— 50 —| |— 25 —| |— 62 —|

50

25

RULE   DO NOT STRING DIMENSION OUT TO TOTAL OVERALL SIZE

ANSI standards state for standard dimensions, you should suppress your leading zeros.

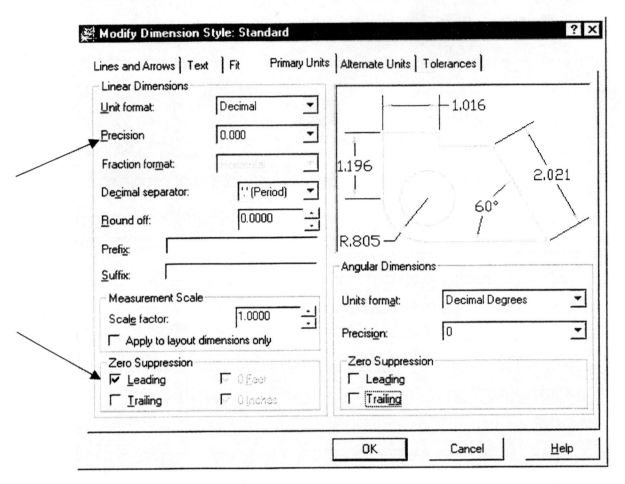

Additionally, you want to keep the precision for your dimensions to three decimal places or less. A good rule of thumb is that every decimal place adds 10% to the cost of fabrication.

Select the Primary Units tab on the Dimension Style dialog box. Set Precision to three places. Enable Zero Suppression next to Leading.

Press OK.

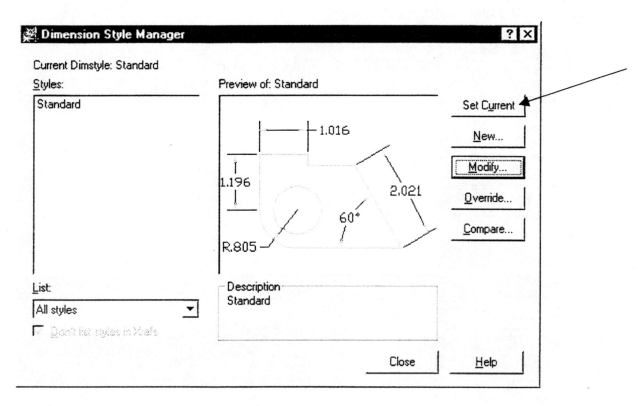

Press the 'Set Current' to save your new settings.
Press 'Close' or ENTER on the keyboard.

If you have existing dimensions in your drawing, they will not reflect your new settings.

To update your existing dimensions:

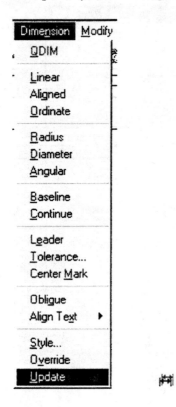

```
Command: _-dimstyle
Current dimension style:  Standard
Enter a dimension style option
[Save/Restore/STatus/Variables/Apply/?] <Restore>: _apply

Select objects:
```

At the select objects prompt, type 'ALL' to select all existing dimensions or pick to select only the dimensions you wish to modify.

Exercise 1:   Gage

Set drawing precision to 2.
Create three layers:

Object	Green
Hidden	Cyan
Dimension	Red

Draw a front, top, and right side view as shown.

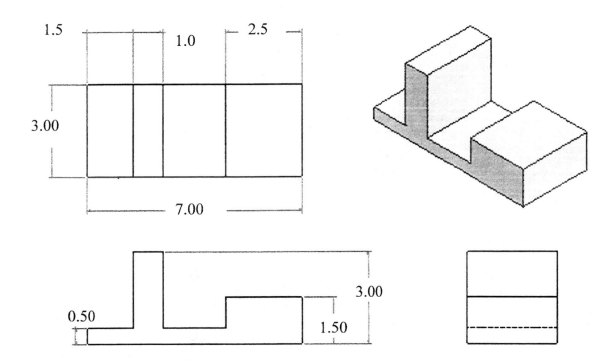

Exercise 2:   Clamp

Set drawing precision to 2.
Create three layers:

Object	Green
Hidden	Cyan
Dimension	Red

Draw a front, top, and right side view as shown.

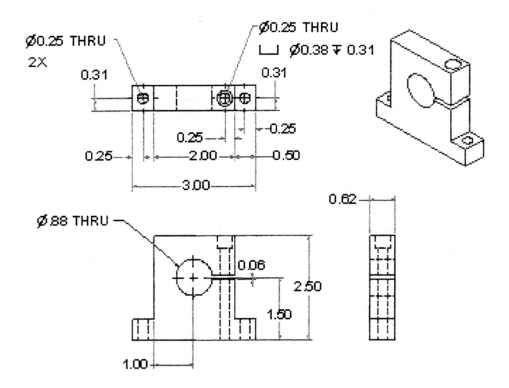

Lesson 6
Auxiliary Views

Learning Objectives:

- ANSI Standards for Auxiliary View
- How to draw/create an auxiliary view

AUXILIARY VIEWS HAVE THE FOLLOWING CHARACTERISTICS:

- SHOWS THE TRUE SHAPE/SIZE OF A FEATURE

- USED TO DIMENSION FEATURES THAT ARE DISTORTED IN PRINCIPAL VIEWS

- PROJECTED PERPENDICULAR FROM THE REFERENCE PLANE

AUXILIARY VIEW CONVENTIONS

- HIDDEN LINES ARE NOT SHOWN UNLESS THEY CLARIFY THE VIEW

- THE VIEW IS PLACED USING THE SAME DISTANCE (~ 2.5 UNITS) FROM THE REFERENCE VIEW AS THE OTHER VIEWS

- THE VIEW MUST BE PERPENDICULAR TO THE REFERENCE PLANE

- ONLY SHOWS THE PROJECTED PLANE

OTHER FACTS ABOUT AUXILIARY VIEWS...

- AN AUXILIARY VIEW MAY REDUCE THE NEED FOR PRINCIPAL VIEWS OF THE PART

- A PARTIAL AUXILIARY VIEW CAN BE USED IF IT REVEALS THE NECESSARY FEATURES

- YOU CAN HAVE AN AUXILIARY VIEW OF AN AUXILIARY VIEW

HOW TO DRAW AN AUXILIARY VIEW IN AUTOCAD

STEP 1: DRAW THE FRONT & TOP VIEWS

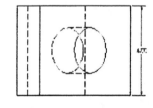

NOTE HOW THE HOLE IS DISTORTED ON THE TOP VIEW.

SINCE THE HOLE IS ON AN INCLINED SURFACE,

AN AUXILIARY VIEW IS THE BEST WAY TO SHOW THE DETAIL.

STEP 2: DETERMINE THE ANGLE OF THE INCLINED SURFACE

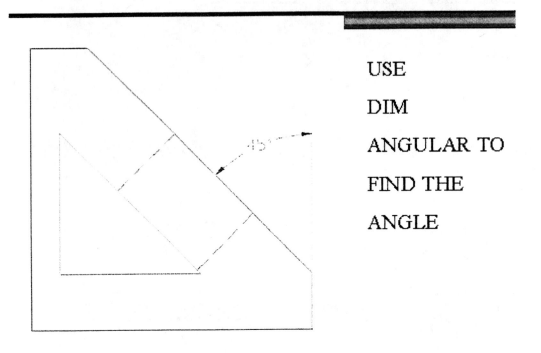

USE

DIM

ANGULAR TO

FIND THE

ANGLE

Command: SNAP

Specify snap spacing or

[ON/OFF/Aspect/Rotate/Style/Type] <0.5000>: R

Specify base point <0.0000,0.0000>: _endp of (PT1)

Specify rotation angle <0>: 45

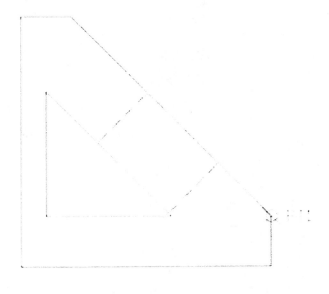

STEP 3:

Set SNAP to

the angle
determined

STEP 4: DRAW CONSTRUCTION LINES TO
MAP OUT THE VIEW

USE OFFSET

TO GET THE
CORRECT WIDTH
OF THE OBJECT

NOTE: ONLY
PROJECT THE EDGES
OF THE INCLINED
SURFACE

POSITION THE AUXILIARY VIEW SO THAT IT
WILL NOT INTERFERE WITH THE DIMENSIONS

STEP 5: TRIM THE PROJECTION LINES TO CREATE THE OBJECT OUTLINE

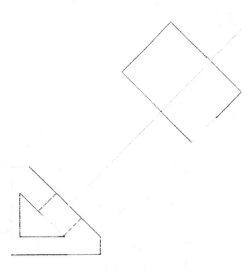

STEP 6: OFFSET ONE OF THE EDGES TO LOCATE THE HOLE

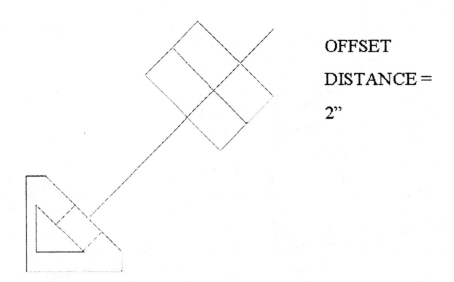

OFFSET

DISTANCE =

2"

STEP 7: DRAW HOLE USING CONSTRUCTION LINES

HOLE DIA = 2"

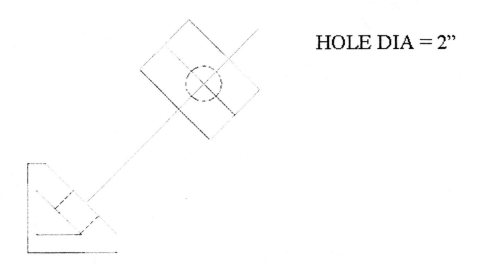

STEP 8: DELETE CONSTRUCTION LINES

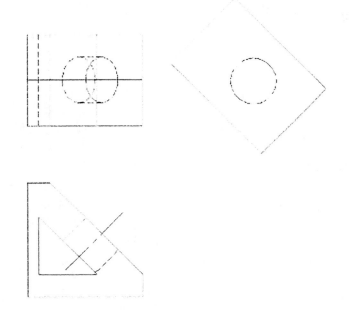

STEP 9: PLACE DIMENSIONS FOR AUXILIARY VIEW

USE THE ROTATE OPTION

TO PLACE THE DIMENSIONS

Command: _dimlinear
First extension line origin or press ENTER to select: _endp of
Second extension line origin: _cen of
Dimension line location
(Mtext/Text/Angle/Horizontal/Vertical/Rotated): R
Dimension line angle <0>: 45
Dimension line location
(Mtext/Text/Angle/Horizontal/Vertical/Rotated):
Dimension text = 2.50

Exercise 1: Auxiliary View

Set drawing precision to 2.
Create three layers:

Object	Green
Hidden	Cyan
Dimension	Red

Create three views:
Front, Right Side and Auxiliary

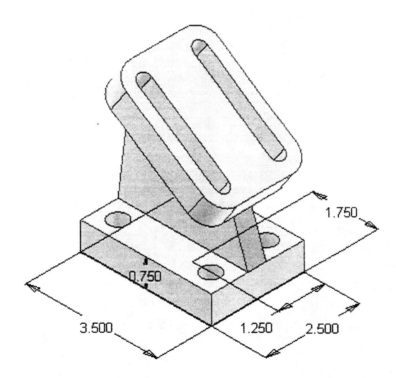

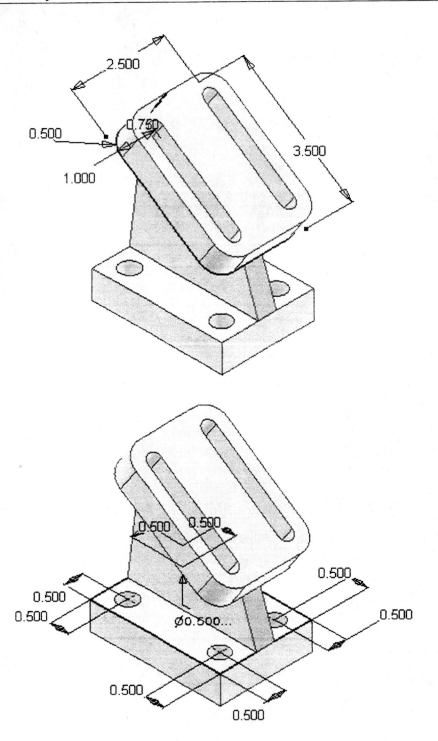

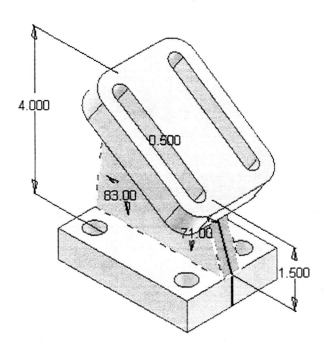

Holes are .50 dia thru.
Slots are concentric to the fillets.
Slots are .50 dia x 2.5.
Fillets are R.50.

Exercise 2: Auxiliary

Set drawing precision to 2.
Create three layers:

Object	Green
Hidden	Cyan
Dimension	Red

Create three views:
Front, Right Side and Auxiliary

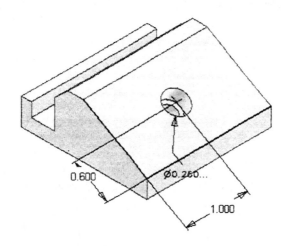

Hole is Counterbore 0.375 x 0.25 DP
0.250 THRU

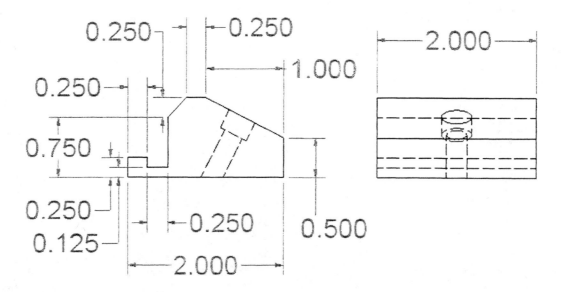

TITLE BLOCKS

Lesson 7
Title Blocks

Learning Objectives:

- How to insert a title block
- How to create attributes
- How to edit attributes

Technical drawings require a title block and a border.

You will notice that there are four arrows on the border, one on each side. The arrows are a leftover from the days when technical drawings were done on vellum. Drafters would create drawings using multiple sheets. Each sheet would act as a layer. The arrows were used to line up the views so that the overlays would match.

Most companies have a title block template that contains their company name and logo, as well as company address and contact information. As drafters, you need to know how to create and modify title blocks in case the company information changes and how to insert title blocks for use in your drawings.

STANDARD DRAWINGS COME IN SEVERAL SIZES....

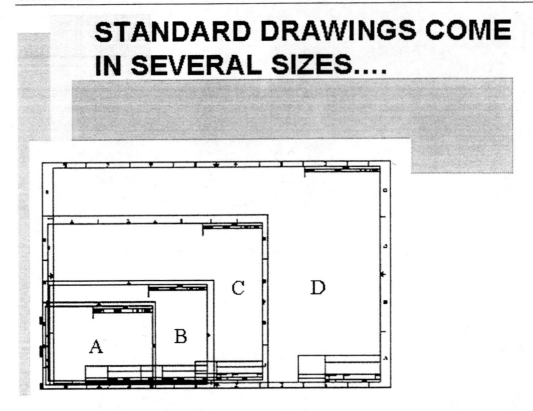

In AutoCAD, all models and views are drawn 1:1. That way we can compare parts to make sure they fit together. In order to plot, we scale the title block and then scale the plot.

Each title block size is double the previous size...

A SIZE: 8-1/2 X 11

B SIZE: 11 X 17

C SIZE: 17 X 22

D SIZE: 22 X 34

Contents of 'Template'

Name	Size	Type
ANSI A title block (portrait).dwg	28KB	AutoCAD Drawing
ANSI A title block.dwg	28KB	AutoCAD Drawing
ANSI B title block.dwg	28KB	AutoCAD Drawing
ANSI C title block.dwg	30KB	AutoCAD Drawing
ANSI D title block.dwg	31KB	AutoCAD Drawing
ANSI E title block.dwg	32KB	AutoCAD Drawing
Architectural Title Block.dwg	27KB	AutoCAD Drawing
DIN A0 title block.dwg	29KB	AutoCAD Drawing
DIN A1 title block.dwg	29KB	AutoCAD Drawing
DIN A2 title block.dwg	29KB	AutoCAD Drawing
DIN A3 title block.dwg	29KB	AutoCAD Drawing
DIN A4 title block.dwg	30KB	AutoCAD Drawing
Generic 24in x 36in Title Block.dwg	27KB	AutoCAD Drawing
ISO A0 title block.dwg	36KB	AutoCAD Drawing
ISO A1 title block.dwg	35KB	AutoCAD Drawing
ISO A2 title block.dwg	33KB	AutoCAD Drawing
ISO A3 title block.dwg	33KB	AutoCAD Drawing
ISO A4 title block (portrait).dwg	32KB	AutoCAD Drawing
JIS A0 title block.dwg	35KB	AutoCAD Drawing
JIS A1 title block.dwg	34KB	AutoCAD Drawing
JIS A2 title block.dwg	34KB	AutoCAD Drawing
JIS A3 title block.dwg	33KB	AutoCAD Drawing
JIS A4 title block (landscape).dwg	32KB	AutoCAD Drawing
JIS A4 title block (portrait).dwg	31KB	AutoCAD Drawing

AutoCAD comes with standard title block templates. They are located in the Template subdirectory under AutoCAD. The location on your computer will depend on where you loaded AutoCAD.

By adding attributes to a title block, we can easily modify the text values and we can later learn how to export the attribute values to create a database for our parts drawings.

AN ATTRIBUTE IS A TAG ATTACHED TO A BLOCK

ATTRIBUTES ARE USED:

- TO STORE INFORMATION

- ALLOW FOR EASIER EDITING

- EXTRACT INFORMATION FOR DATABASES OR SPREADSHEETS

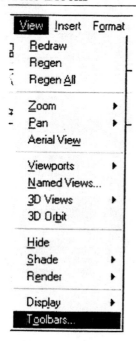

The toolbar icons to create and edit attributes are not located on the Draw or Modify toolbars. We can access them by customizing our existing toolbars.

Go to View-> Toolbars in the menu.

You can also access the Toolbars Customize dialog by right clicking in the top gray area of the screen. Right click and select Customize.

ADD THE TOOLBAR ICONS
YOU NEED....

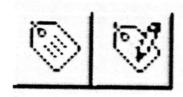

DEFINE ATTRIBUTES

EDIT ATTRIBUTES

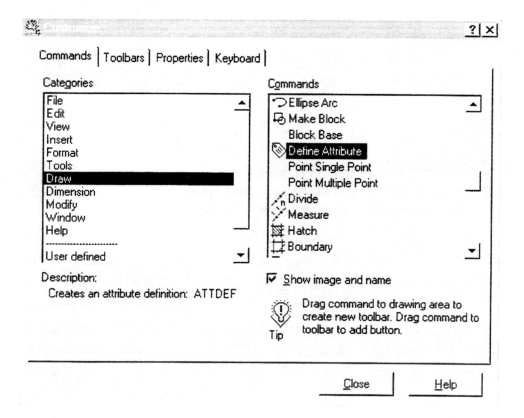

Select the Commands Tab.
Select the Draw Category.
Scroll down to see the Define Attribute tool.
With the left mouse button, drag the Define Attribute tool to the existing Draw toolbar to add it.

TIP: Some of the icons may not be familiar to you. If you left pick on the button, a description of what it does will appear in the bottom left of the dialog box.

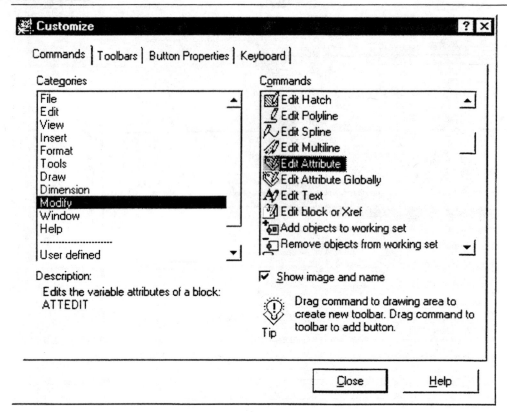

Select the Modify Category.
Scroll down to the Edit Attribute Command.
With the left mouse button, drag the Edit Attribute tool to the existing Modify toolbar to add it.

There are three ways to define an attribute:

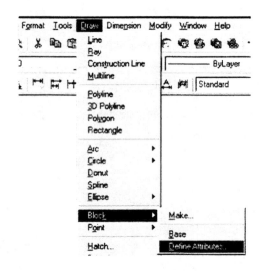

```
Command: DDATTDEF

Initializing...   DDATTDEF loaded.
```

Menu	Draw->Block->Define Attributes
Toolbar	Customize
Command Line	DDATTDEF

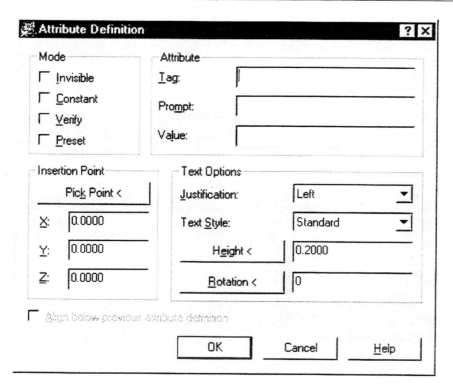

The Attribute Definition dialog box appears.

There are four modes of Attribute definitions:

- Invisible
- Constant
- Verify
- Preset

Invisible attributes are used to store information in a drawing that is not seen in normal mode. Some companies will create a set of invisible attributes that list the layer standards. Drafters then turn the attribute display on so they can see the layer standards and turn them off when they are ready to plot their drawings. Other companies use invisible attributes to store cost information for parts. They don't want the customer to see how much the material costs, but they need the information to estimate project costs.

Constant attributes are used when the value does not change, such as company name, but the information is needed for extraction to a database.

Verify mode prompts the user with a Yes/No after they enter the attribute value to give them a chance to recheck their entry.

Preset sets the attribute to its default value when you insert a block containing a preset attribute.

TIP: To control the display of attributes use the command ATTDISP. Normal is normal/default viewing mode. ON allows you to see invisible and visible attributes. OFF makes all attributes invisible.

We're going to define a title block with attributes that we can then use on all drawings.

☞ Select Open file.

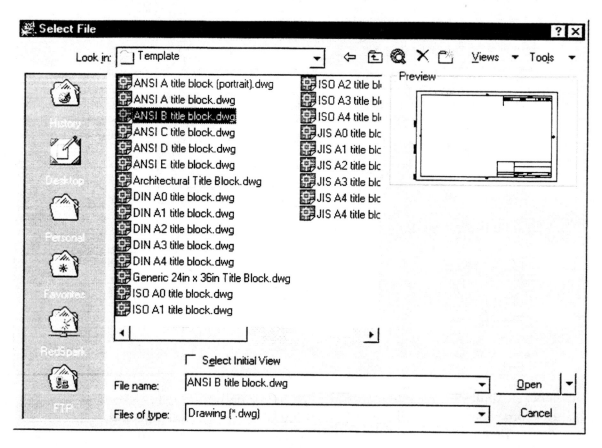

Locate ANSI B title block.dwg in the Template directory.

Create the attributes in the table below:

TAG	PROMPT	VALUE	X	Y	HEIGHT	MODE
DRAFTER	DRAFTER	(YOUR INITIALS)	9.5	0.75	0.125	
DATE	DATE	8/23/99	9.5	0.5	0.125	
COMPANY	COMPANY	COLLEGE NAME	11.25	1.75	0.1575	CONSTANT
SIZE	SIZE	B	11.25	0.7	0.125	
REV	REV	A	15	0.7	0.125	
SCALE	SCALE	1/1	11.6	0.4	0.125	
SHEETNO	SHEET NO	1 OF 1	14	0.4	0.125	
DWGNO	DWG NO	PX-X	12.75	0.7	0.125	
DWGNAME	DWG TITLE	NOUN, ADJECTIVE	11.25	1.2	0.25	
FILENAME	FILE NAME	PX-X	11.6	0.7	0.125	

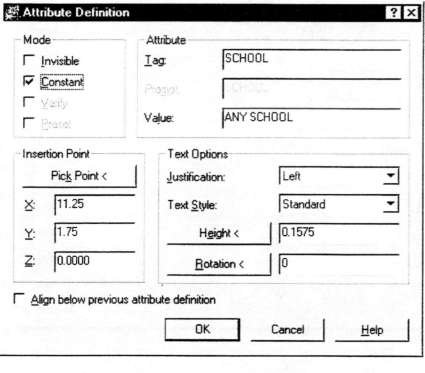

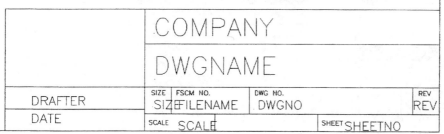

Your title block should look like this. You'll notice that some of the attributes don't fit properly in the title block. This is OK. The values will fit just fine.

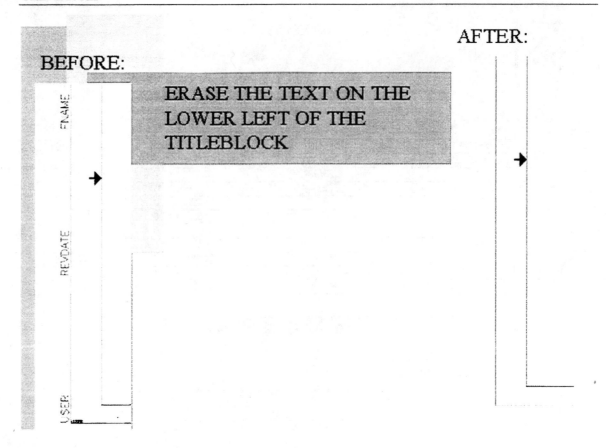

Erase the pre-defined attributes in the title block.

Adding a Logo

Many companies like to see their logo in the title block. AutoCAD allows you to insert graphics into drawings.

Any gif, jpg, bmp, etc. can be inserted. For this lesson, we will use the logo for our college.

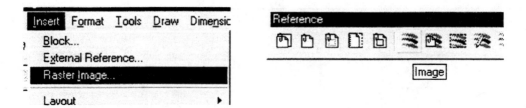

You can insert a graphic image using the menu or the image tool located on the Reference toolbar.

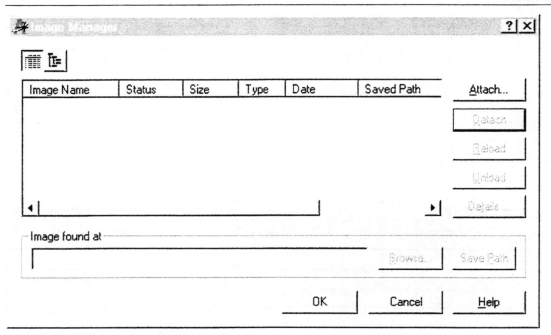

The Image Manager dialog box appears.
Press the 'Attach' button.

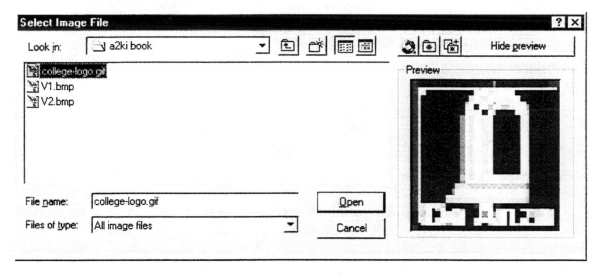

A dialog box will come up. Browse for the desired graphic file and select Open.

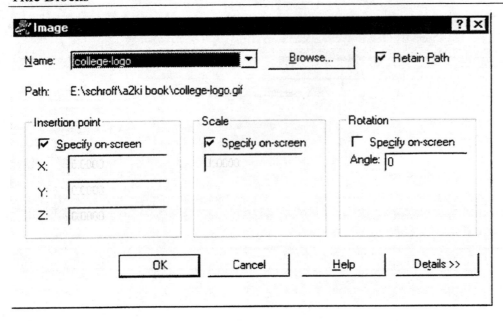

We specify the insertion point and scale on screen. We enable the Retain Path option, so our graphic will automatically update if the graphic is modified at a later date.

Press 'OK'.

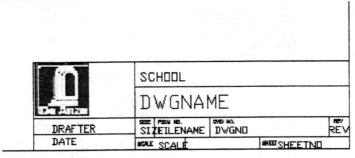

Locate the graphic as shown.

If we use the menu to insert our graphic, we will not see the Image Manager dialog box, but will immediately go to the browse dialog box to locate our image file.

Save Drawing As

Perform a Save Drawing As and save the drawing as ansi_b_{your initials} in your working directory.

TIP: It is a good idea to save any custom blocks, toolbars, etc. in a separate directory away from AutoCAD. That way you can easily back up your custom work to use on another work station and if you need to reinstall AutoCAD for any reason, you will not lose your work.

☐ Start a New Drawing using English Units.

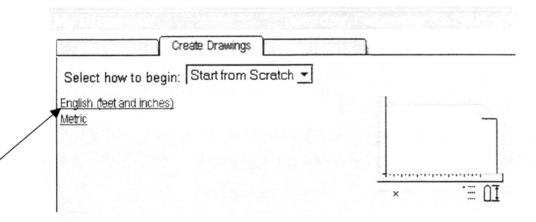

Now, we will insert our title block.

To insert a title block, you have three methods:

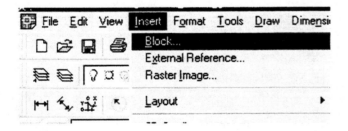

Command: DDINSERT

Menu	Insert-> Block
Draw Toolbar	Insert Block
Command Line	DDINSERT

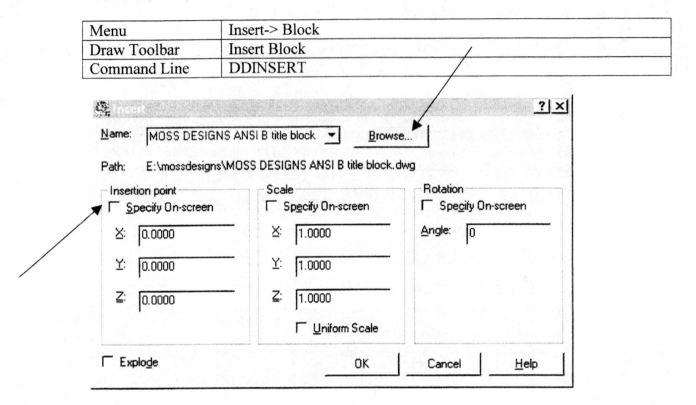

Locate your title block using the Browse button.
If you deselect the Specify On-Screen button under Insertion point, the title block will automatically insert at the origin (0,0).

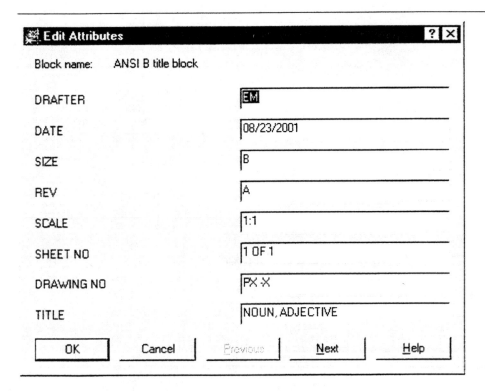

A dialog box will appear to prompt you for the attributes you defined.

Fill it out and press 'OK'.

TIP: If you were prompted on your command line for the attribute values instead of in a dialog box, then you need to reset your ATTDIA system variable. Type ATTDIA at the command line and enter '1'. This will enable the dialog box for attributes.

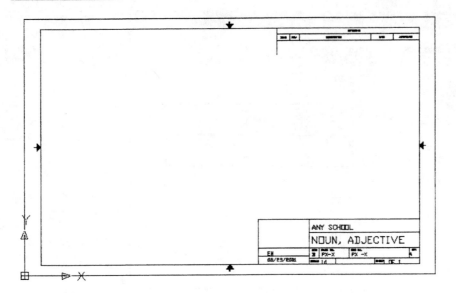

Your title block will appear in your drawing.

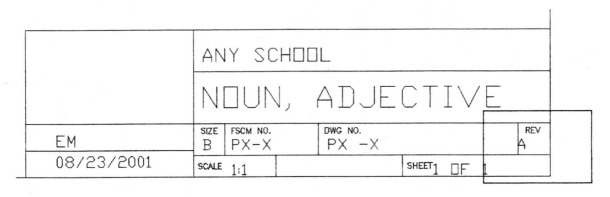

The 'A' under Rev is needs to be moved slightly.

We can modify attributes in-place using –ATTEDIT.

```
Command: -ATTEDIT

Edit attributes one at a time? [Yes/No] <Y>:   <ENTER>

Enter block name specification <*>:  <ENTER>

Enter attribute tag specification <*>:    <ENTER>

Enter attribute value specification <*>:    <ENTER>
Select Attributes: 1 found
Select Attributes:          <ENTER>

1 attributes selected.
Enter an option [Value/Position/Height/Angle/Style/Layer/Color/Next] <N>: P

Specify new text insertion point <no change>:   <Pick a new location >
Enter an option [Value/Position/Height/Angle/Style/Layer/Color/Next] <N>:    <ENTER>
```

To change the values of any of the attributes, use Edit Attribute.

Edit Attribute can be accessed three ways:

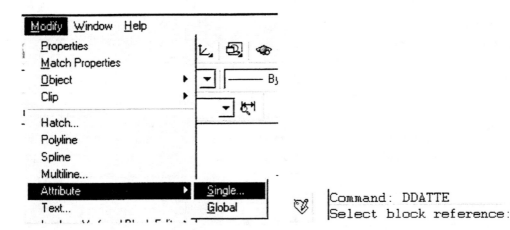

Menu	Modify->Attribute->Single
Toolbar	Customize to access Edit Attribute
Command Line	DDATTE

Select the title block.

The dialog box will appear to give you access to all the attribute values.

If your title block is too small or large for your drawing views, use SCALE to scale the title block. Always SCALE in multiples of 2. Remember each ANSI drawing size is double the size of the previous size. Never scale your views to fit into your title block.

If you are plotting a B size drawing to an A size sheet of paper, you will scale your plot by half.

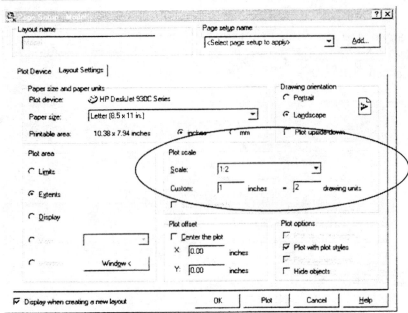

A good rule of thumb when plotting is that the plot scale is the inverse of the scale of the title block…

When plotting to an 81/2 x 11 size sheet of paper:

A size title block	1:1
B size title block	1:2
C size title block	1:4
D size title block	1:8

When plotting to an 11 x 17 size sheet of paper:

A size title block	1:2
B size title block	1:1
C size title block	1:2
D size title block	1:4

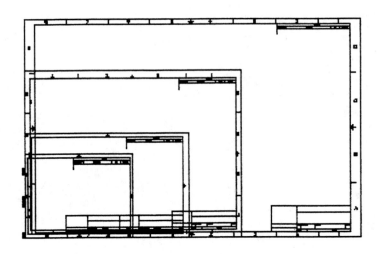

QUIZ 2

1. Which dimensioning unit is most often used for Mechanical technical drawings?

    A. Decimal
    B. Engineering
    C. Architectural
    D. Scientific

2. The Define Attribute tool is located on the Draw toolbar. (T/F)

3. A group of dimension variables with specified settings is termed a dimension style. (T/F)

4. The icon shown is:

    A. INSERT BLOCK
    B. BINSERT
    C. MAKE BLOCK
    D. WBLOCK

5. The ____ option of the PLINE command is used to switch from drawing polylines to drawing polyarcs and provides options associated with the drawing of polyarcs.

    A. POLYARC
    B. ARC
    C. ELLIPSE
    D. SWITCH

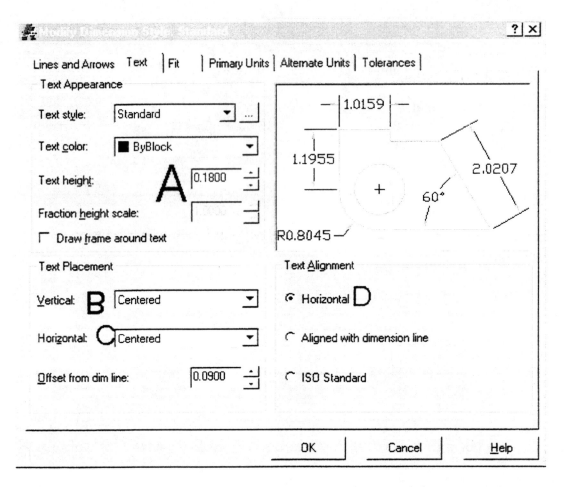

6. SELECT THE AREA OF THE DIMENSION FORMAT DIALOG BOX DESIGNED
    TO SET DIMENSION TEXT ABOVE THE DIMENSION LINES

7. A polyline can be converted to a line.   (T/F)

8. The icon shown is:

    A. Edit Label
    B. Edit Text
    C. Edit Attribute
    D. Write Attribute

9. You set the precision in the Units dialog box shown. What precision does that control?

    A. Coordinates for data entry and in the coordinate display in the lower left hand of the
    screen
    B. The number of decimal places in dimensions
    C. The number of decimals you need to enter for coordinate entry
    D. The size of the limits

10.   Dimensions cannot be updated.   (T/F)

11.   Most drawing layouts in the U.S. consist of TOP VIEW, BOTTOM VIEW, AND LEFT-SIDE VIEW.   (T/F)

12.   What is the most frequently used dimensioning standard

    A.   ASME
    B.   ISO 9000
    C.   ANSI
    D.   Decimal

13.   The icon shown is:

    A.   CIRCLE, DIA
    B.   DIMDIAMETER
    C.   CIRCLE, 2P
    D.   DIMLINEAR

14.   Dimension Styles cannot be named.   (T/F)

15.   The icon shown is:

    A.   Define Attribute
    B.   Edit Attribute
    C.   DDedit
    D.   Label

16.   Attributes are defined as:

    A.   Database information displayed by entering the LIST command
    B.   Coordinate information
    C.   Informational text associated with a block
    D.   MTEXT

17.   The icon shown is:

    A.   Insert Block
    B.   WBLOCK
    C.   Make Block
    D.   Insert Image

18.   A block is:

        A.   A rectangular shaped object
        B.   A single LEGO piece
        C.   One or more entities stored as a single object for later retrieval and insertion
        D.   A selection set of entities

19.   A command used to edit attibutes is:

        A.   DDATTE
        B.   EDIT
        C.   ATTFILE
        D.   EDITATT

20.   The layout used for drawings in the US and Canada is called FIRST ANGLE
        PROJECTION.   (T/F)

21.   The default dimension style is called:

        A.   DEFAULT
        B.   STANDARD
        C.   OVERRIDE
        D.   STYLE1

22.   The _____ dialog box is used to control dimension styles and variables.

        A.   DIMENSION
        B.   DIMSTYLE
        C.   Dimension Style Manager
        D.   STYLE

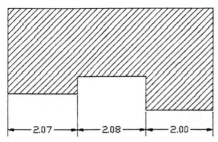

2.07   2.08   2.00

23.   The command used to dimension the image illustrated above is

    A.   BASELINE
    B.   CONTINUE
    C.   RADIAL
    D.   ORDINATE

24.   To turn ORTHO mode ON, press:

    A.   F7
    B.   F8
    C.   F9
    D.   F10

25.   Objects in AutoCAD should be drawn 1:1.   (T/F)

ANSWERS:

1) A; 2) F; 3) T; 4) A; 5) B; 6) C; 7) T; 8) C; 9) A; 10) F; 11) F; 12) ANSI; 13) B; 14) F;
15) A; 16) C; 17) C; 18) C; 19) A; 20) F; 21) B; 22) C; 23) B; 24) B; 25) T

Notes:

Lesson 8
Hole Annotation

Learning Objectives:

- ANSI Standards for Hole Annotation
- Dimensioning Holes
- Drawing holes

One of the most common mistakes students make is in dimensioning and labeling holes. ASME has defined how holes are to be labeled to ensure proper fabrication.

The most common holes used in fabricated parts are:

- Drill/Ream
- Counterbore
- Countersink

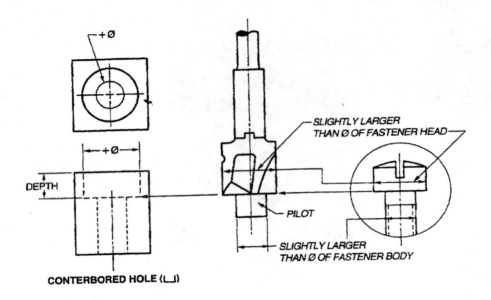

Counterbore holes are drawn in a symbolic fashion.

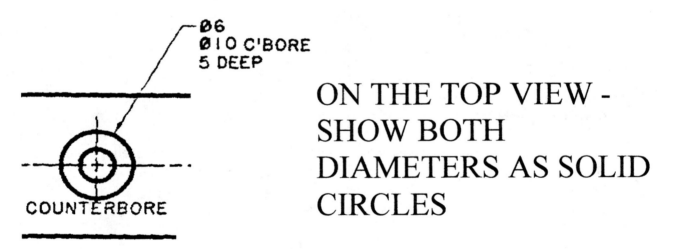

ON THE TOP VIEW - SHOW BOTH DIAMETERS AS SOLID CIRCLES

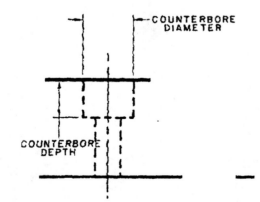

ON THE SIDE VIEW - SHOW COUNTER BORE DEPTH - USE HIDDEN LINES

A common error is to forget the hidden depth line.

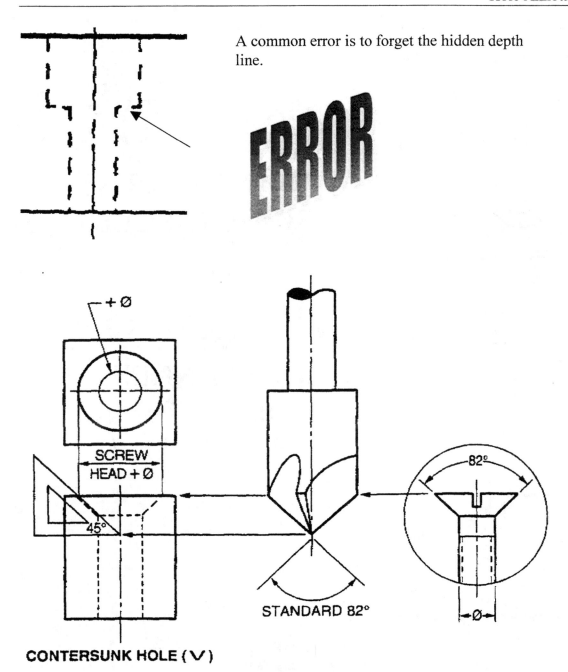

ERROR

CONTERSUNK HOLE (∨)

Countersunk holes are also drawn in a symbolic manner.

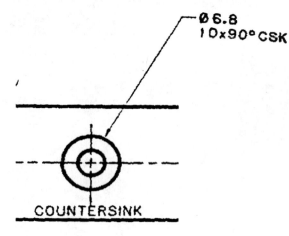

COUNTERSINK

ON TOP VIEW-
SHOW BOTH
DIAMETERS AS
SOLID CIRCLES

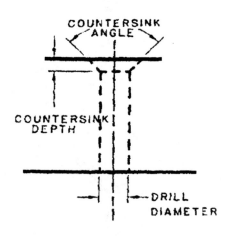

ON SIDE VIEW-
SHOW ANGLE
& DEPTH OF
COUNTERSINK

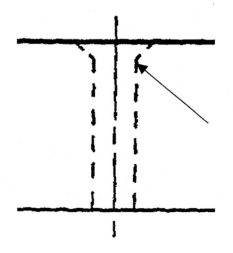

A common error is to forget the hidden depth line.

Drawing a Drill hole

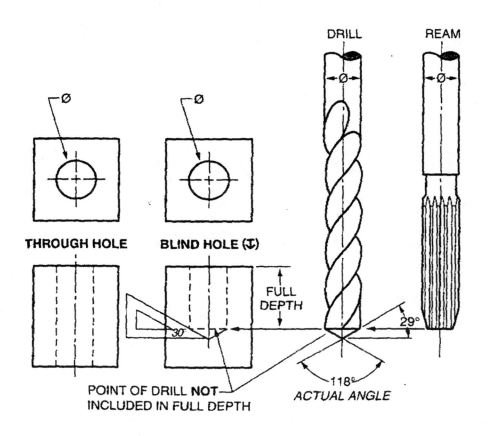

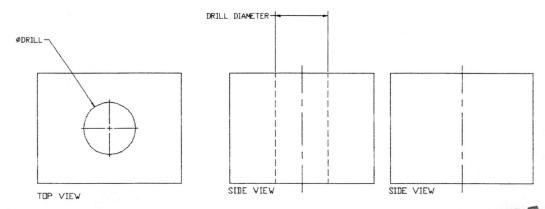

NOTE: USE
CONTINUOUS
LINETYPE IN TOP
VIEW

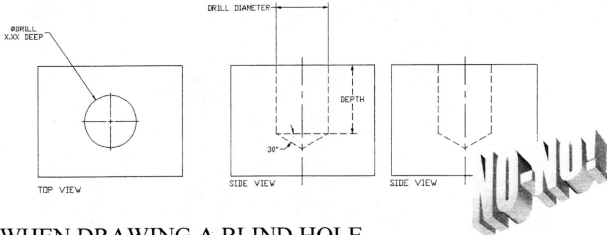

WHEN DRAWING A BLIND HOLE,
SHOW THE DEPTH OF THE HOLE IN
SIDE VIEW-
USE HIDDEN LINES

When dimensioning holes, follow these rules:

- Always use hole diameter – NOT radius
- Always note whether it is blind or through
- Always note the depth of blind holes
- Always note the depth of counterbores
- Always note the angle of countersinks
- Label using the order of operation

We use the hole diameter NOT the radius because the drill bits used by the machine shops are labeled by diameter. If you label a hole using a radius, there are two possible outcomes:

Outcome #1:   The fabricator will call you to verify the dimension. If this happens, your company will be charged for the additional labor and it will result in a schedule delay.

Outcome #2:   The fabricator will assume that you meant the number to be a diameter and will drill the holes too small. The parts will come in wrong and will need to be reworked. Your company will have to pay for the additional expense and it will result in a delay.

ANSI standards state that it is optional to label through holes as THRU. The drawing should be clear enough that the fab house can see it is a through hole. However, it is important to eliminate any chance of a drawing being misread, so I recommend to my students to label holes THRU if they are through or provide a depth if they are blind. That way there can be no mistakes.

Students often get confused when dimensioning counterbore and countersink holes as to the order of annotation. Which do you put first the diameter for the body or the diameter for the counterbore? Always label in order of operation. The machinist always drills the body hole first and then the hole for the counterbore/countersink. Consider the hole annotation as instructions to the machinist in how to drill the hole.

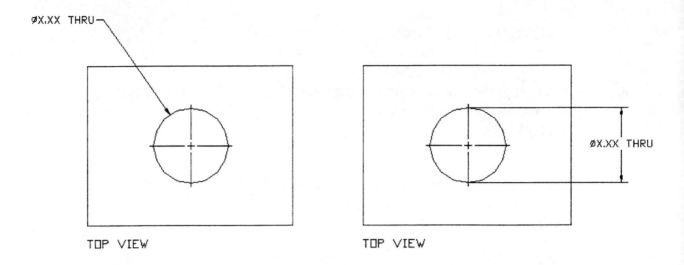

Holes should be dimensioned on the top view using a diameter. Both views shown are correct.

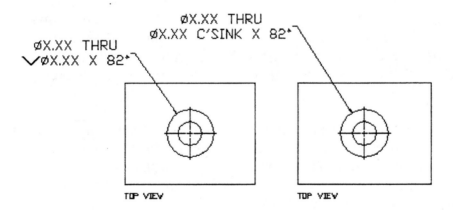

When labeling a countersink hole, you can use either a countersink symbol or the word C'SINK.

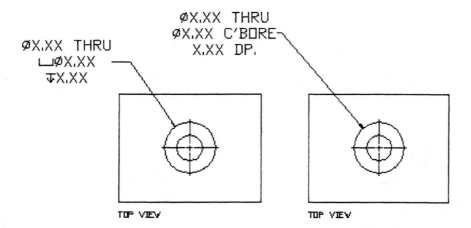

When labeling a counterbore hole that has a through body, you can label as shown above. You can use the word C'BORE or the counterbore symbol. For the depth of the counterbore, use the depth symbol or the word DP.

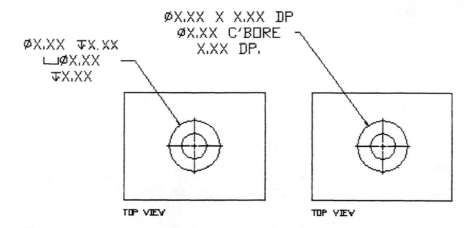

For blind holes, use the annotation shown above.

To access the hole annotation symbols, follow the instructions below.

Start the DIMDIAMETER command.

Place the dimension.

Modify the dimension.

(Located on the Modify II toolbar)

```
Command: ed
DDEDIT
Select an annotation object or [Undo]:
```

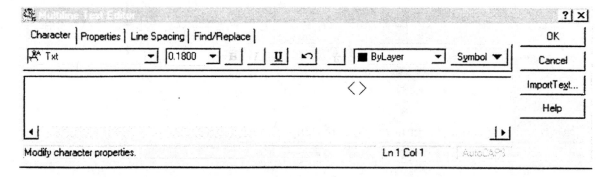

The Multiline Text Editor appears. You see ◇ inside the edit box. The ◇ indicate the associated dimension value.

TIP: If you accidentally delete your dimension value, you can restore it by typing ◇.

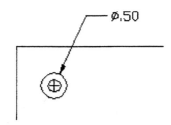

Let's assume that we are dimensioning a counterbore hole with a diameter of 0.25 thru for the body, a counterbore diameter of 0.50 and a counterbore depth of 0.125. The associative dimension we see in the edit box is for the counterbore dimension. We need to place the thru hole dimension in front of the counterbore diameter.

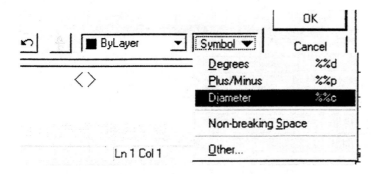

Under the Symbol dropdown, we see Diameter in the list.
You see %%c next to diameter. The %%c is a fallback from the old days of text and DOS. %%c is an ASCII code to create a diameter symbol. %%d is used to create a degree symbol. They used the letter 'c' because the letter 'd' was taken for degree and 'c' indicates 'circle'.

Select Diameter. Type .25 THRU next to it as shown.

We need to add a counterbore symbol in front of the counterbore diameter.

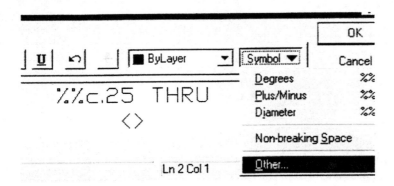

Select 'Other'.

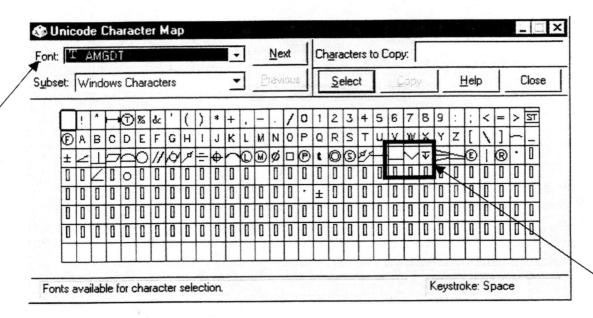

Set the Font to AMGDT and GDT.
The hole symbols are located in the character list right next to each other.

Left pick the box with the counterbore symbol located on the left of the countersink symbol.

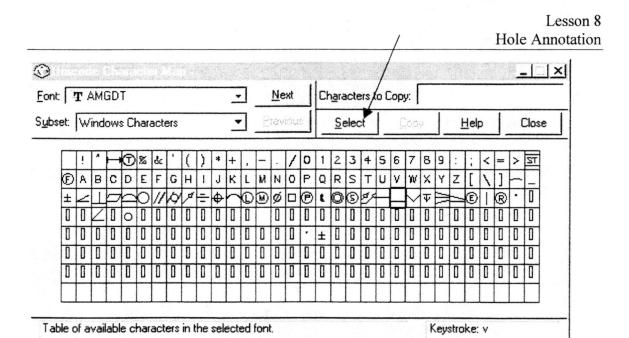

An outline will appear around the counterbore box. Press the Select button.

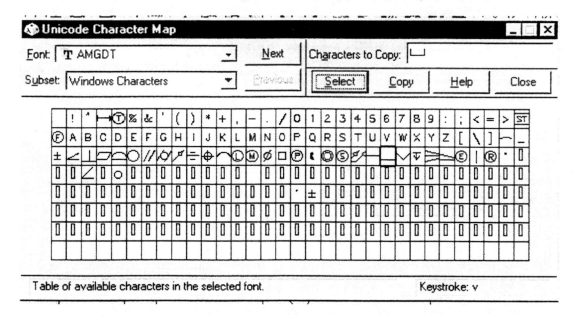

The counterbore symbol will appear in the Characters to Copy box.
Press the Copy button.
Then Close.

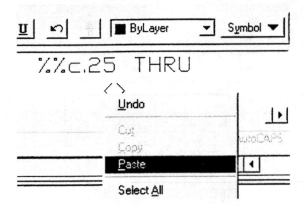

Locate your mouse in front of the ◇.
Right click and select Paste.

The counterbore symbol will be placed.

Repeat the process to add the depth note.

If you highlight the symbols, you will note that the text height is different from the text.
This will cause the annotation to look odd when you plot.

Highlight the entire text and set it to a standard height.

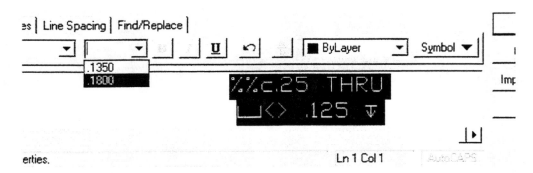

Press 'OK'.

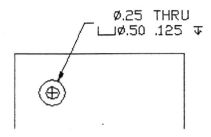

Exercise 1:

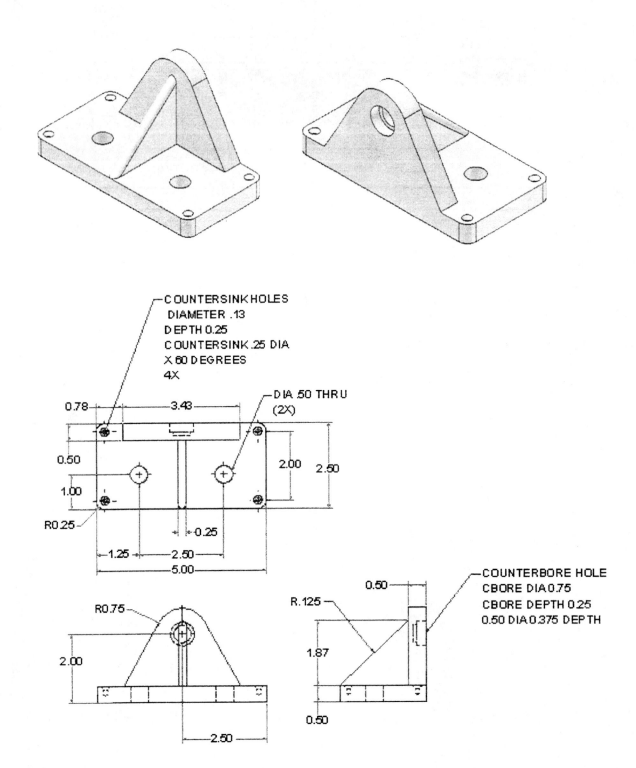

COUNTERSINK HOLES
 DIAMETER .13
DEPTH 0.25
COUNTERSINK .25 DIA
X 60 DEGREES
4X

DIA .50 THRU
(2X)

0.78

3.43

0.50

1.00

2.00

2.50

R0.25

0.25

1.25

2.50

5.00

COUNTERBORE HOLE
CBORE DIA 0.75
CBORE DEPTH 0.25
0.50 DIA 0.375 DEPTH

R0.75

2.00

2.50

R.125

0.50

1.87

0.50

Use proper hole annotation.

8-16

Lesson 9
Templates

Learning Objectives:

- Creating Templates
- Using Templates

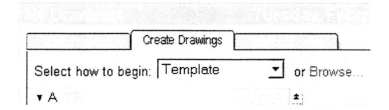

One of the options when you Create a Drawing is to use a template. Many companies set up and use templates to ensure their drafters comply with their internal standards. Templates are great because you only need to set up your layers, title blocks, and dimension styles once.

VARIABLES THAT CAN BE SET IN YOUR TEMPLATE

- •LAYERS

- •DIMSTYLES

- •TEXTSTYLES

- •BLOCKS

- •UNITS

- •LIMITS

A good way to decide what you want to set up in your template is to think about what items you set up whenever you start a new drawing. Create a check list.

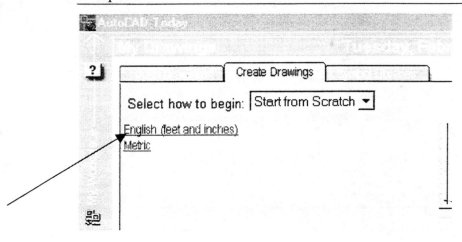

Start your template by selecting Start from Scratch and English from the Create Drawings tab.

SET UP YOUR LAYERS

LAYERS:

DIMS

OBJECT

CENTER

HIDDEN

NOTES

TITLEBLOCK

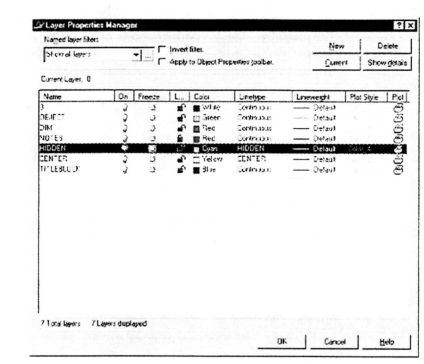

SET UP YOUR DIMSTYLE

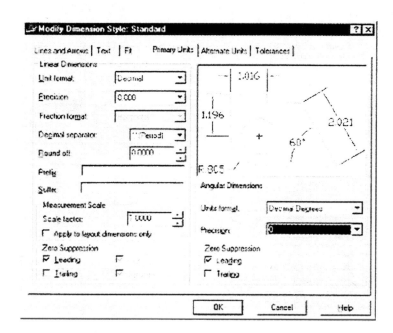

SET YOUR
PRECISION TO 3
FOR LINEAR AND
0 FOR ANGULAR.

SUPPRESS
LEADING ZEROS

SET YOUR LIMITS

LIMITS

FROM 0,0 TO 34,22

GRID SPACING 1"

STORE A BLOCK

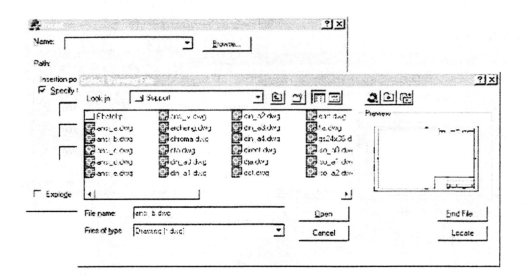

USE INSERT & FIND THE TITLEBLOCK YOU WANT
TO USE WITH YOUR DRAWINGS...WHEN YOU SEE
THE PROMPT FOR THE INSERTION PT - HIT ESC!

TIP: By pressing ESC you don't actually place the block. Instead you are storing it locally in the drawing, so you don't have to browse for it when you are ready to insert it.

Make any other settings you want to complete your template.

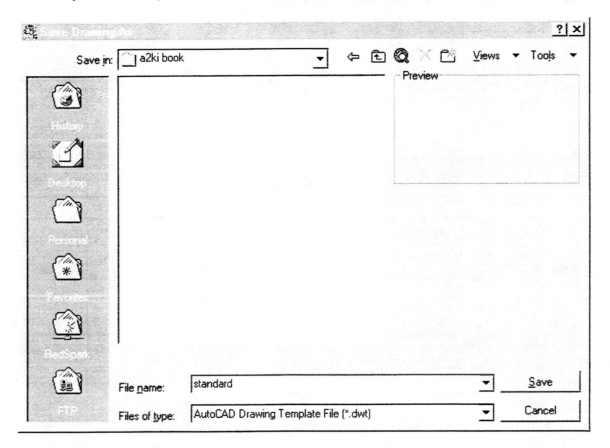

Select Save Drawing As.

Under Files of Type, select AutoCAD Drawing Template (*.dwt).

Store your template in a directory away from AutoCAD – NOT in the Template subdirectory. That way you can back up and copy your template to a different work station as needed.

Call your template 'standard'.

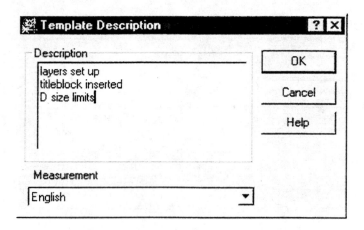

You can enter a description of your template in the Description box. To drop down a line, press Control and ENTER.

Press 'OK'.

Close your template.

Test your template...

Start a New File.

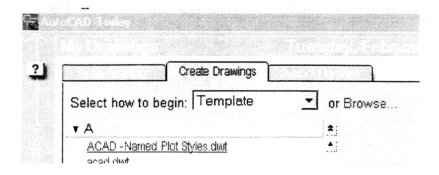

Select Template from the drop down and select Browse.

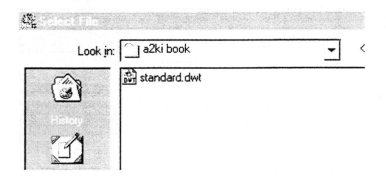

Locate your template in the directory you selected.

Press 'Open'.

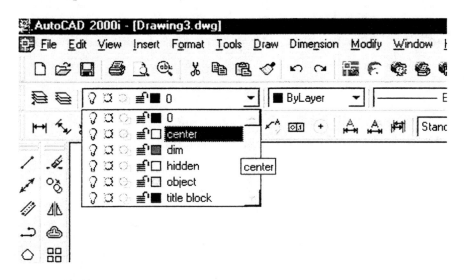

Check that your layers are set up.

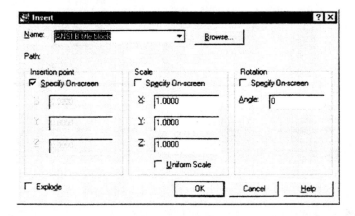

And when you go to insert a block, your title block is ready to go!

Templates

- Allow you to pre-setup your drawings

- Save you time

- Boost productivity

- Just load and go!

Lesson 10
Isometric Views

Learning Objectives:

- Using Draft Settings to create Isometric Views
- Creating Isometric Circles

WHAT IS AN ISOMETRIC DRAWING?

•A 2D DRAWING IN A 2D PLANE

•AIDS IN VISUALIZING THE SHAPE OF THE OBJECT

•USED IN ASSEMBLY DRAWINGS

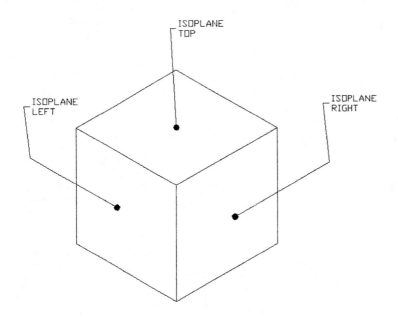

AutoCAD uses three isoplanes to create an isometric view.

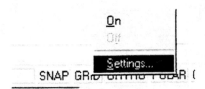

SNAP GRID ORTHO POLAR (

To switch your cursor to draw isometric, place your mouse over the GRID/SNAP button on the bottom of the screen. Right click and select Settings.

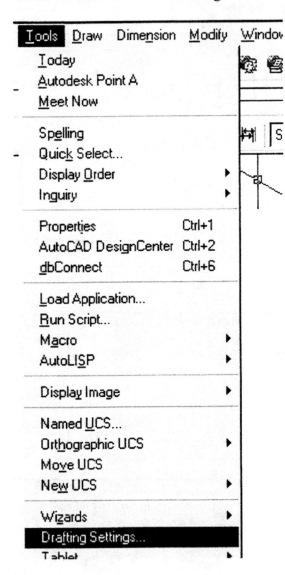

You can also access the Drafting Settings dialog by using Tool->Drafting Settings

Snap type & style

    ⊙ Grid snap

        ○ Rectangular snap

        ⊙ Isometric snap

    ○ Polar snap

Enable Isometric snap.

```
Command: snap
Specify snap spacing or [ON/OFF/Rotate/Style/Type] <0.5000>: s
Enter snap grid style [Standard/Isometric] <I>:
```

You can also switch to isometric mode on the command line by typing Snap, S, I

The methods to switch to isometric mode:

Menu	Tools->Drafting Settings
GRID/SNAP	Right click to access Settings
Command line	SNAP, S, I

Note how the cursor has changed to isometric mode.

TO SET ISOPLANE

Command line: isoplane

Left / Top / Right / <Toggle>: Enter an option or press ENTER

Ctrl-E is a shortcut

You can toggle between isoplanes three ways:

Command line	ISOPLANE
Shortcut key	Ctrl-E
Function key	F5

How to draw an isometric figure

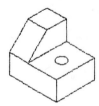

Step 1:   Set ORTHO ON.
Step 2:   Set Isoplane to Left.

Step 3. USE ORTHO TO INDICATE THE DIRECTION
YOU WANT THE LINE TO GO...

Command: _line
From point: 10,6
To point: 2.5
To point: 1
To point: 2.5
To point: c

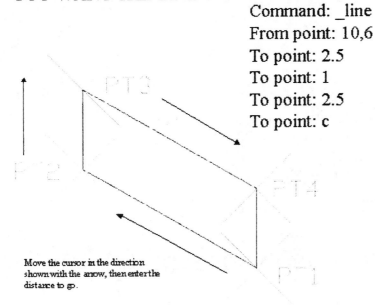

Move the cursor in the direction
shown with the arrow, then enter the
distance to go.

Step 4. Switch to Isoplane Right
using Control-E

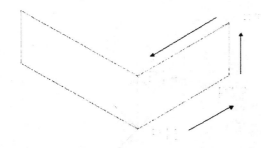

Command: _line From point: _endp of (PT1)
To point: 2 (PT2)
To point: 1 (PT3)
To point: _endp of (PT4)
To point:

Step 5. Switch to Isoplane Top Using Ctl-E

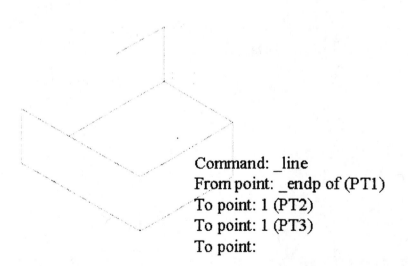

```
Command: _line
From point: _endp of  (PT1)
To point: 1.5 (PT2)
To point: 2.0 (PT3)
To point:
```

Step 6. Switch to Isoplane Right Ctl-E

```
Command: _line
From point: _endp of (PT1)
To point: 1 (PT2)
To point: 1 (PT3)
To point:
```

Step 7. Switch to ISOPLANE
TOP- CTL-E

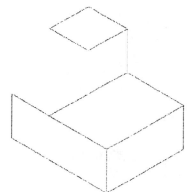

Command: _line Specify first point: _endp of
Specify next point or [Undo]: 1.0
Specify next point or [Undo]: 1.0
Specify next point or [Close/Undo]: _endp of

Step 8. Draw lines from endpoint
to endpoint to create the inclined
surface.

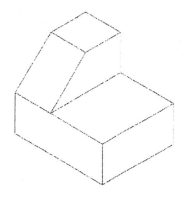

Step 9. To draw an isometric circle - Use ellipse - Isometric

Ctrl- E to the plane where you want to place the circle

Use tracking to locate the circle

Command: ELLIPSE
Specify axis endpoint of ellipse or
[Arc/Center/Isocircle] : i
Specify center of isocircle: tk
First tracking point: _mid
Next point (Press ENTER to end tracking): _mid
Next point (Press ENTER to end tracking):
Specify radius of isocircle or [Diameter]: 0.25

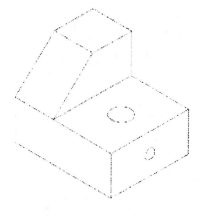

Exercise 1:

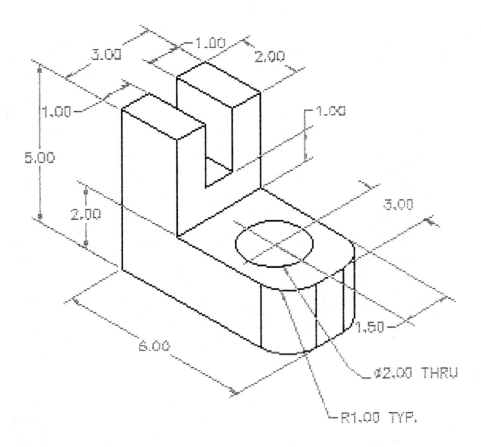

Create three orthographic views, plus an isometric.
Use standard layers and title block.

Exercise 2:

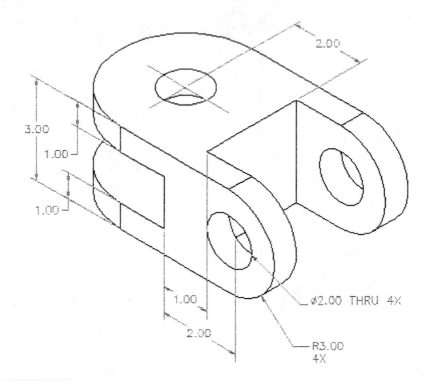

Create three orthographic views, plus an isometric. Use standard layers and title block. Part is symmetric.

Lesson 11
Section Views

Learning Objectives:

- Hatching
- How to draw a cutting plane line
- Section Views

Before you can create a section view, you need to understand how to add and modify hatch patterns.

There are three methods to create Hatch patterns:

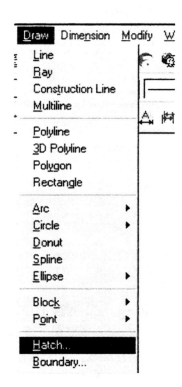

Command: bhatch

Menu	Draw-> Hatch
Draw Toolbar	
Command line	BHATCH
Shortcut	H

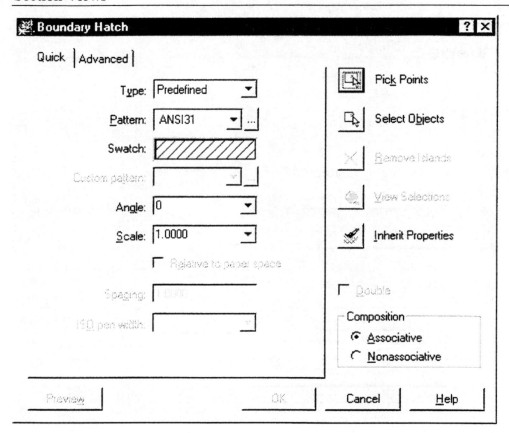

Hatches are associative by default. This means that if you stretch the boundary, the hatch will stretch and adapt with it.

Section hatching should be placed on a separate layer. That way you can turn off hatching to speed up regen time. You want to assign a light line weight as well.

The first hatch pattern should be placed at 45 degrees. Other hatch patterns are opposed to the original hatch pattern.

Once you have placed a hatch pattern, you can edit using the HATCHEDIT command.

There are three methods to access the HATCHEDIT command:

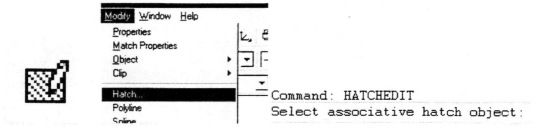

Menu	Modify ->Hatch
Modify II Toolbar	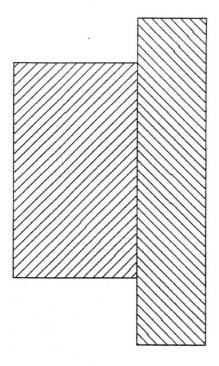
Command Line	HATCHEDIT
Shortcut	HE

You have more than one hatch pattern in a section view to illustrate different parts or materials.

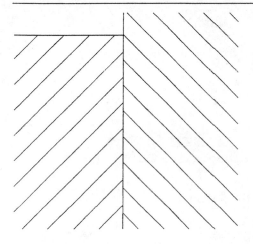

If you look closely at the patterns, you notice that they don't match up.

You can use the command SNAPBASE to line up the patterns.

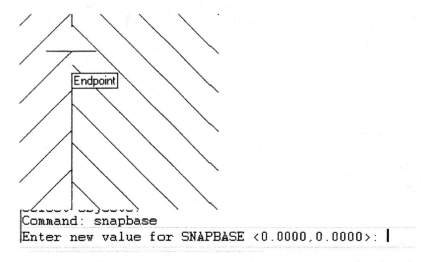

Type SNAPBASE at the command line when prompted for the new value select the endpoint of the existing hatch.

Select Hatchedit, pick the hatch pattern to align, and then press 'OK'.

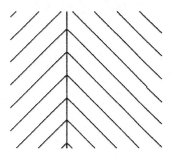

The hatch patterns are now aligned.

Section views are used to reveal interior features that cannot be shown in standard orthographic views.

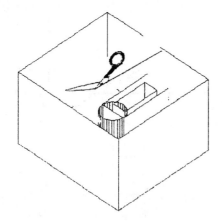

PASS AN IMAGINARY CUTTING PLANE THROUGH THE PART, PERPENDICULAR TO THE LINE OF SIGHT

The cutting plane line represents the edge of the imaginary cutting plane. The direction of the arrows indicate the direction of sight.

Creating a cutting plane line is easy with the polyline command.

Cutting plane lines should be placed on a separate layer. Load a dashed linetype.

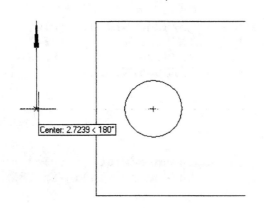

Use object tracking to line up your cutting plane with the center of any holes.

Start the pline command.
The arrow is created with a starting width of zero and ending width of 0.1. The arrow length should be no more than .5 units. The line width should be set to 0.04.

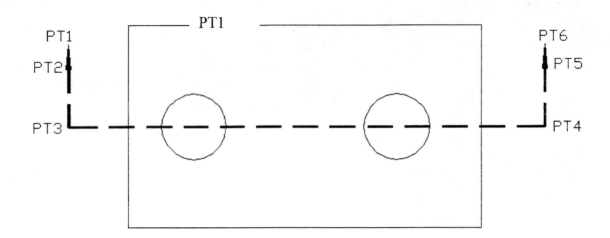

```
Command: _pline
Specify start point: (PT1)
Current line-width is 0.0000
Specify next point or [Arc/Halfwidth/Length/Undo/Width]: W

Specify starting width <0.0000>:

Specify ending width <0.0000>: 0.1

Specify next point or [Arc/Halfwidth/Length/Undo/Width]: 0.5 (PT2)

Specify next point or [Arc/Close/Halfwidth/Length/Undo/Width]: W

Specify starting width <0.1000>: 0.04

Specify ending width <0.0400>: 0.04

Specify next point or [Arc/Close/Halfwidth/Length/Undo/Width]: (PT3)
Specify next point or [Arc/Close/Halfwidth/Length/Undo/Width]: (PT4)
Specify next point or [Arc/Close/Halfwidth/Length/Undo/Width]: (PT5)
Specify next point or [Arc/Close/Halfwidth/Length/Undo/Width]: W

Specify starting width <0.0400>: 0.1

Specify ending width <0.1000>: 0.0

Specify next point or [Arc/Close/Halfwidth/Length/Undo/Width]: (PT6)
Specify next point or [Arc/Close/Halfwidth/Length/Undo/Width]: <ENTER>
```

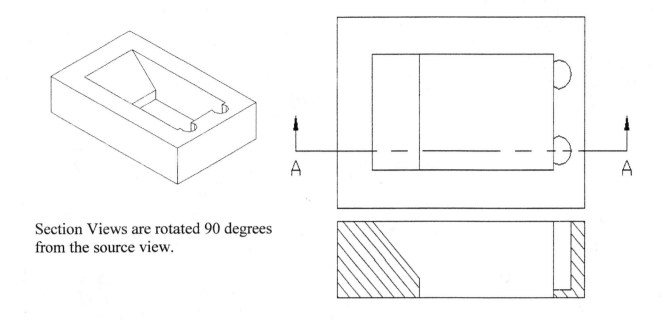

Section Views are rotated 90 degrees
from the source view.

SECTION A-A

SECTION LINES

- ● SECTION LINES ARE THINNER THAN OBJECT LINES

- ●SECTION LINES ARE A DIFFERENT COLOR & LAYER THAN OBJECT LINES

- ● PRIMARY SECTION LINES ARE AT A 45° ANGLE

- ● USE THE COMMAND 'BHATCH' TO CREATE SECTION LINES

- ● ALWAYS PREVIEW THE HATCH BEFORE PLACEMENT

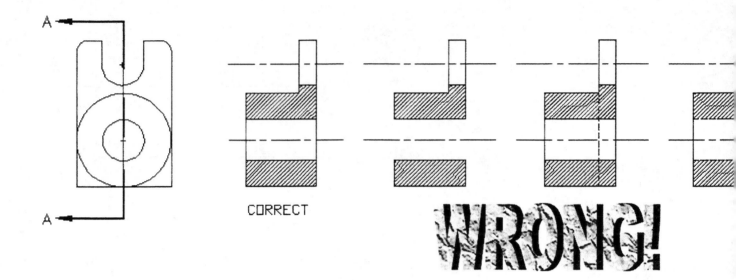

CORRECT

WRONG!

When creating a section view, do not use hidden lines. Imagine the section as though a knife has cut through the part. All edges should be revealed as continuous lines.

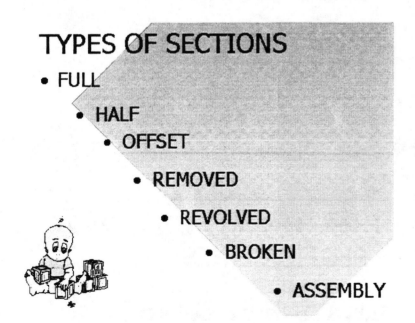

TYPES OF SECTIONS
- FULL
- HALF
- OFFSET
- REMOVED
- REVOLVED
- BROKEN
- ASSEMBLY

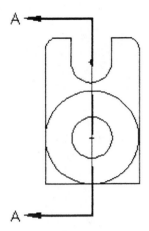

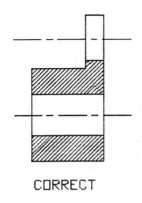

CORRECT

Full Sections are the most common type of section views.

Cutting plane extends through the entire part, in a straight line, usually on the centerline of symmetry

Half Section Views are used for symmetrical parts.

One-fourth of the part is "removed" and the interior is exposed.

The line that separates the sectioned half from the non-sectioned half is a centerline

The bottom half of the section may be left blank or be used to show a standard orthographic view with hidden lines.

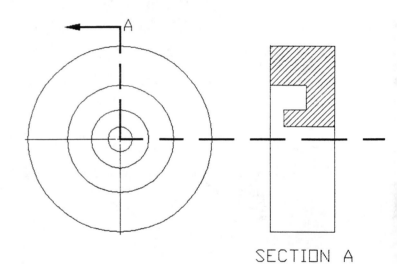

SECTION A

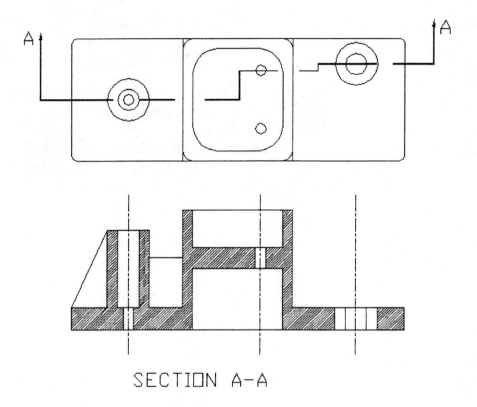

Offset planes are used when features are not in line.

The cutting plane is stepped (offset) at right angles to pass thru features that are not in a straight line

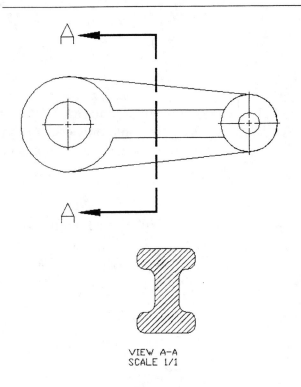

VIEW A-A
SCALE 1/1

A removed section is used to show transitional details.

The section is placed away from other views.

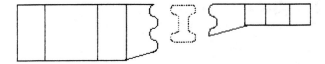

A revolved section uses a broken line instead of a cutting plane line. The broken line is also created using PLINE.

Use the MIRROR command to show the other side of the broken point and then edit the PLINE to make it fit.

A revolved section is shown between the two broken edges.

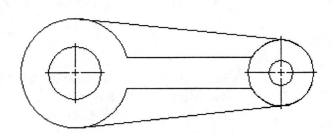

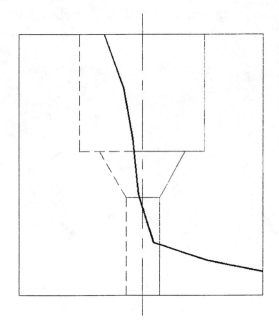

Broken sections are used to reveal interior features. They are commonly used to show the inside of water heaters, insulation, and bed springs.

- Exposes only a small portion of the object
- Use zig-zag polyline to create cut
- No cutting plane line is used

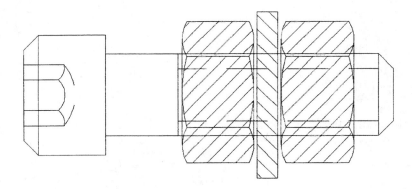

An assembly section is used to show a section view of an assembly. The view displays show two or more parts in assembly. The hatching angle should be changed between the parts in order to distinguish them. The primary or main part should be sectioned with a 45 degree angle. Use SNAPBASE to align the hatch patterns.

POINTS TO REMEMBER

THAT'S A LOT TO REMEMBER!

- SMALL PARTS, SUCH AS BOLTS, NUTS, BALL BEARINGS, ETC. SHOULD NOT BE SHOWN IN SECTION VIEW

- HIDDEN LINES ARE NOT SHOWN IN SECTION VIEWS

- SECTION LINES SHOULD BE LIGHTER THAN OBJECT LINES. TO DO THIS, ALL HATCHING SHOULD BE A DIFFERENT COLOR AND LAYER

MORE POINTS TO REMEMBER

BROKEN LINE (ZIG-ZAG POLYLINE)

USED ON THE FOLLOWING SECTION VIEWS:

- REVOLVED SECTION

- BROKEN

ONLY TWO TYPES OF SECTION VIEWS USE BROKEN LINES!

SUMMARY:

SECTION VIEWS ARE USED TO

SHOW INTERNAL FEATURES

THERE ARE MANY TYPES OF
SECTION VIEWS

SECTION VIEWS USE CUTTING PLANE
LINES OR BREAK LINES.

ALL SECTION VIEWS USE SECTION
LINES.

Exercise 1:
Full Section

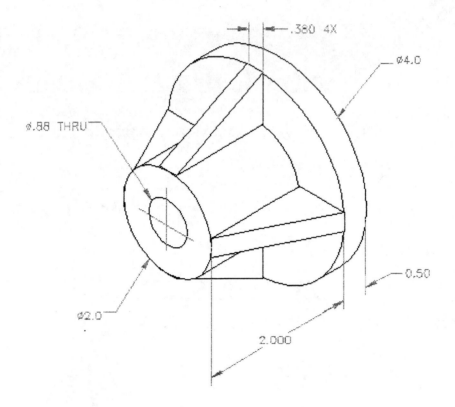

Exercise 2
Half Section

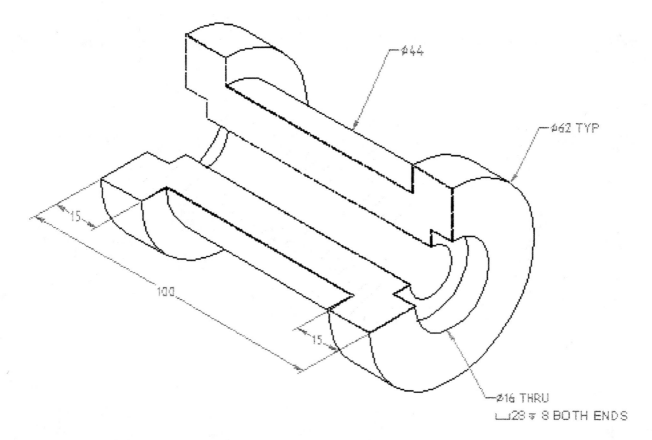

METRIC

Exercise 3
Offset Section

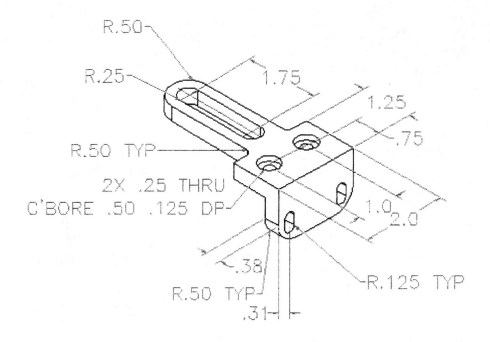

Exercise 4
Removed Section

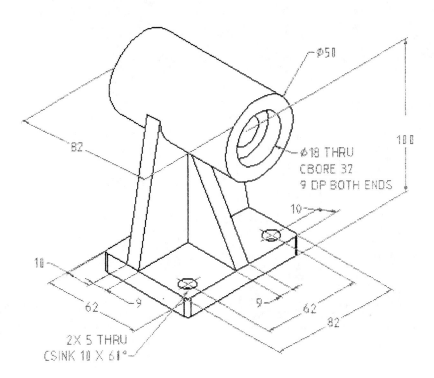

Ø50

Ø18 THRU
CBORE 32
9 DP BOTH ENDS

82

100

10

10

62

9

9

62

82

2X 5 THRU
CSINK 10 X 61°

Exercise 5
Full Section

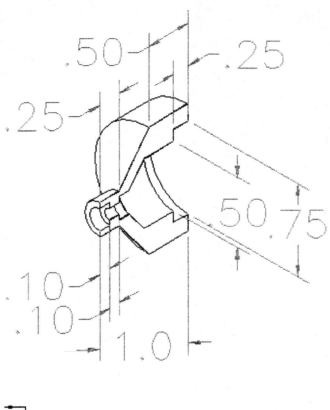

QUIZ 3

1. When mating parts are shown on an assembly drawing, section lining for both parts are done at the same angle. (T/F)

2. To draw a circle in an isometric figure, use:
    A. CIRCLE, SNAP, ROTATE
    B. ELLIPSE, ISO
    C. ARC, ROTATE
    D. ARC, ISO

3. When drawing an isometric figure, the function key used to toggle between ISOPLANES is:
    A. F2
    B. F3
    C. F4
    D. F5

4. Section views can not be used for assembly drawings. (T/F)

5. The section view is rotated 180 degrees out of the cutting plane. (T/F)

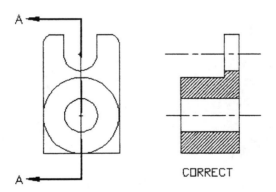

6. The section view shown is:
    A. FULL
    B. HALF
    C. QUARTER
    D. REMOVED

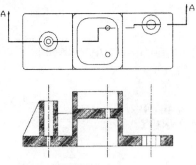

SECTION A-A

7. The section view shown is:
   A. BROKEN
   B. HALF
   C. OFFSET
   D. REVOLVED

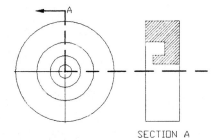

SECTION A

8. The type of section view shown is:
   A. FULL
   B. HALF
   C. OFFSET
   D. REVOLVED

9.   The hot-key to toggle between different ISOPLANES is:
    A.   CTRL-E
    B.   CTRL-A
    C.   CTRL-I
    D.   CTRL-P

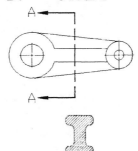

10.   The type of section shown is:
    A.   HALF
    B.   QUARTER
    C.   FULL
    D.   REMOVED

11.   Primary section lines should be drawn at a 30 degree angle.   (T/F)

12.   A cutting plane line
    A.   Indicates the path that an imaginary cutting plane follows to slice
          through an object
    B.   Is used on 3D models
    C.   Indicates where you want to perform a trim
    D.   Indicates where you want to perform an extend

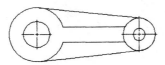

13.   The section view shown is:
    A.   FULL
    B.   OFFSET
    C.   REMOVED
    D.   REVOLVED

14. Hatch patterns are regular patterns of dots, dashes, shapes or lines in a closed area. (T/F)

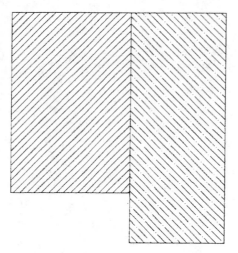

15. To align the hatch patterns as shown, use:
    A. ALIGN
    B. SNAPBASE
    C. ANGLE
    D. HATCHALIGN

16. Section lines should be the same color and linetype as object lines. (T/F)

17. When you increase the scale factor on a hatch pattern, for example scale factor of 2, you see more hatch lines. (T/F)

18. You have just placed a HATCH pattern in your drawing. However, you notice that the spacing of the lines that make up the hatch pattern are closely spaced together. The spacing needs to be increased. To do this, use:
    A. ERASE
    B. SCALE
    C. EXPLODE
    D. HATCHEDIT

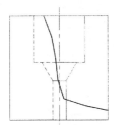

19. The section view shown is:
    - A.   REMOVED
    - B.   REVOLVED
    - C.   BROKEN
    - D.   HALF

20. HATCH is located in the _____ pull-down menu.
    - A.   Draw
    - B.   Modify
    - C.   Tools
    - D.   Format

21. The direction arrows of a cutting plane line indicate the line of sight.   (T/F)

22. To control the visibility of hatch patterns, you can thaw or freeze the hatch layer. An alternative is to use the FILL command. To turn hatch visibility ON, type:
    - A.   FILL, ON
    - B.   FILL, ENABLE
    - C.   FILL, OFF
    - D.   FILL, YES

23. Section views should have hidden lines.   (T/F)

ANSWERS:
1) F; 2) B; 3) D; 4) F; 5) F; 6) A; 7) C; 8) B; 9) A; 10) D; 11) F; 12) A;
13) D; 14) T; 15) B; 16) F; 17) F; 18) D; 19) C; 20) A; 21) T; 22) A; 23) F

NOTES:

FASTENERS

Lesson 12
Fasteners

Learning Objectives

- Specifying fasteners
- Selecting a fastener
- Annotating a fastener

There are three basic methods used to assemble parts:

- Adhesives
- Welding
- Fasteners

Method of Assembly

Welding is used when similar materials need to be permanently joined

Adhesives are used for dissimilar materials to be permanently joined and for sealing.

Fasteners join components - whether similar or not - and provide the ability to take apart later

Fasteners are Popular!

About 70% of all joints are connected using fasteners

Fasteners add 5 percent to the cost of assembly

More than 500,000 types of standard fasteners are available today.

Americans use nearly 200 billion fasteners annually -

26 billion in the automotive industry alone

FASTENER SELECTION

Design for Manufacturability (DFM) suggests:

- Use off-the-shelf, readily available standard fasteners

  - Use the minimal number of fasteners in the design

    - Design for ease of assembly and ease of maintenance

What do fasteners do?

Hold/fasten separate parts together

Transmit power, such as opening/closing a faucet

Used to measure or move a part

Screw Threads

A thread is a helical or spiral groove formed on the outside or inside of a cylinder.

A die is used to cut external threads.

A tap is used to cut internal threads

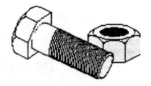

Thread Forms

The thread form is the profile of the thread (the shape of the thread - rectangular, triangular, etc.)

The type of thread form serves different purposes.

ACME or SQUARE threads transmit power, such as opening or closing a valve.

KNUCKLE threads are used for the base of a light bulb, bottle or jar tops.

ANATOMY OF A FASTENER

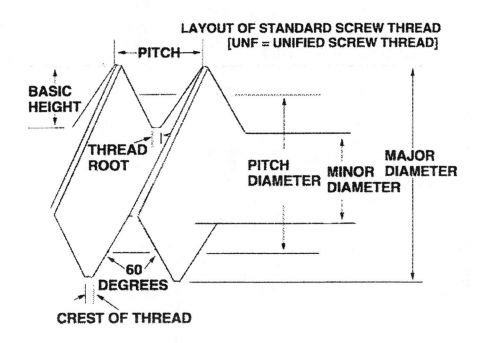

LAYOUT OF STANDARD SCREW THREAD
[UNF = UNIFIED SCREW THREAD]

PITCH

BASIC HEIGHT

THREAD ROOT

PITCH DIAMETER

MINOR DIAMETER

MAJOR DIAMETER

60 DEGREES

CREST OF THREAD

FIT - tightness/looseness between mating parts

Thread Length

(D = diameter of fastener)

For steel - minimum length of engagement = D

For cast iron - minimum length of engagement = 1.50xD

For bronze/zinc - minimum length of engagement = 2.0xD

For aluminum - minimum length of engagement = 2.5xD

Thread Form

3 Major choices:

• UNC

• UNF

• SI

Thread Class

External thread classes:

1A, 2A, 3A

Internal thread classes:

1B, 2B, 3B

The higher the class, the tighter the fit...3 is the tightest

90% of all commercial and industrial fasteners are 2A and 2B

How to annotate threads on a drawing

.250 - 20 UNC-2A

.250 = nominal diameter

20 = number of threads per inch

UNC = thread form

2 = class number

A = external thread

HOW TO DRAW A THREAD IN DRAFTING

THREE METHODS -

- SCHEMATIC

- SIMPLIFIED

- DETAILED

SCHEMATIC

The schematic method is used only for external threads or sectioned internal threads, NOT for internal nonsectioned threads

INTERNAL

EXTERNAL

DETAILED

The detailed is an approximation of the actual appearance of the screw threads. This is the hardest type of fastener representation and is usually reserved for more artistic types of applications.

EXTERNAL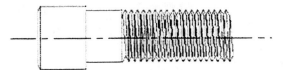

Set up construction lines

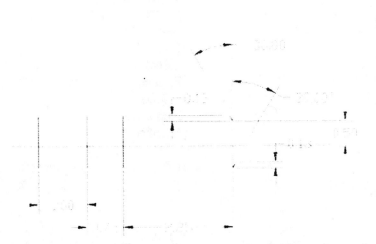

Set up a construction line set

Add thread

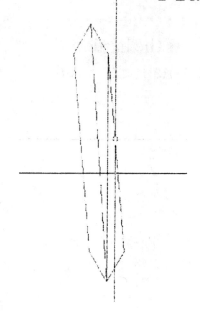

Draw this shape by
using mirror, copy and
line

Array to add threads

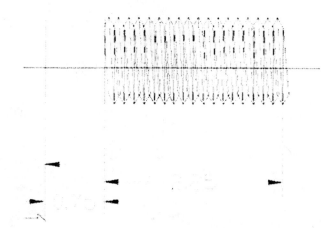

Command: _array
Select objects: w
Select objects: Other corner:
8 found
Select objects:
Rectangular or Polar array
(<R>/P):
Number of rows (---) <1>:
Number of columns (|||)
<1>: 18
Distance between columns
(|||): -0.125

Add head of fastener

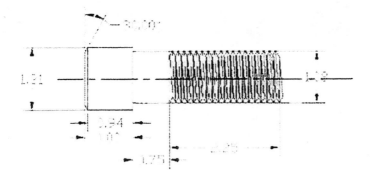

You will need to do some
editing to clean up the area
between the head & the
threads

Notes:

Lesson 13
Assemblies

Learning Objectives

- Design criteria for detail drawings
- Design criteria for assembly drawings
- How to create an item balloon
- How to create a parts list using blocks and attributes
- How to create a parts list using an EXCEL spreadsheet
- Use of XREFs

Up until now, we have concentrated on detail drawings. A detail drawing is a drawing of a single part or component. Another type of drawing is an assembly drawing.

Assembly drawings are used for:

- Ordering Materials
- Assembly instructions
- Packaging
- Determining Cost

Detail drawings are used for:

- Inspection of Parts
- Fabrication Information
- Order Materials

Detail drawings:

- Show the dimensions for the part
- Indicate material and finish
- Fabrication instructions

They are meant to be used without any additional explanation.

Assembly drawings:

- Have a Bill of Materials (list of parts shown in the drawing)
- Show the relationship between the parts
- Identifies the parts (with item balloons)

Assembly drawings do not show dimensions EXCEPT:

- To indicate assembled position
- To show overall dimensions to assist in selecting packaging

Hidden lines are generally not shown in assembly drawings. If you need to show internal features or parts, use a section view.

Small parts, such as bushings and bearings are not shown, except in a detail (close-up) view of the assembly. They may still be indicated in the parts list and with an item balloon.

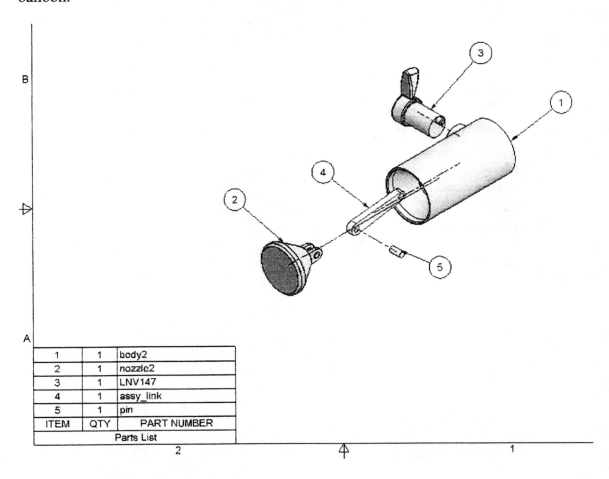

ITEM	QTY	PART NUMBER
1	1	body2
2	1	nozzle2
3	1	LNV147
4	1	assy_link
5	1	pin

Parts List

Parts lists are located so that the parts list heading is on the bottom and the numbers go in ascending order as shown. This makes it easier for someone to add more components to the parts list.

General Notes

General Notes on a drawing are used to supply information that cannot be presented any other way.

General Notes should be:

- All capital text
- In Present Tense
- Oriented horizontally not vertically

General Notes should NOT:

- Be underlined
- Contain abbreviations that are not commonly understood
- Contain information already shown in the dimensions
- Reference something not on the drawing

Place notes in the upper or lower left corner of the drawing.

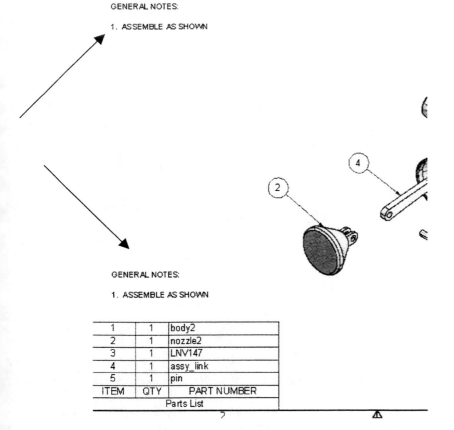

GENERAL NOTES:

1. ASSEMBLE AS SHOWN

GENERAL NOTES:

1. ASSEMBLE AS SHOWN

1	1	body2
2	1	nozzle2
3	1	LNV147
4	1	assy_link
5	1	pin
ITEM	QTY	PART NUMBER
Parts List		

For detail drawings, use notes to:

- Clarify features/dimensions
- Provide fabrication instructions

For assembly drawings, use notes to:

- Provide assembly instructions
- Provide packaging instructions
- Provide maintenance instructions

Creating an Item Balloon

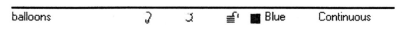

Create a separate layer to place your item balloons.

Use QLEADER to start the leader for the balloon.

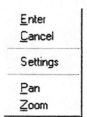

Right click to access the Settings option.

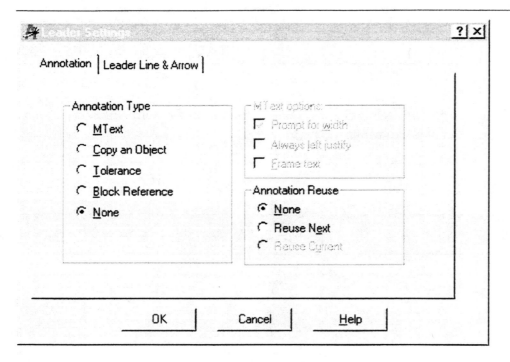

Select the Annotation tab, enable None under Annotation Type.

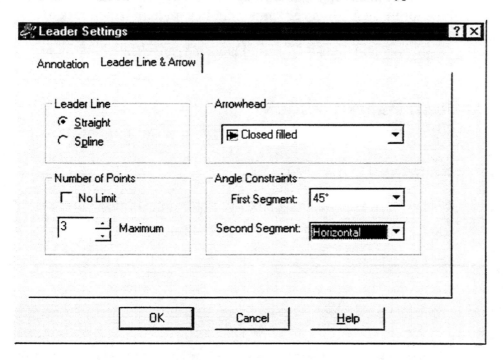

Select the Leader Line & Arrow tab.
Set the Angle Constraints to 45 degrees.
Set the Second Segment to Horizontal.

TIP: You can use the SPLINE option to create curved lines for item balloons. These are commonly used in patent drawings.

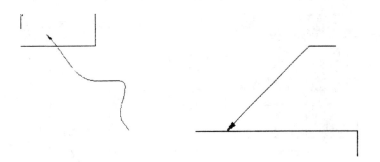

All item balloons should use either text or an attribute. Many drafters create a block with a circle and an attribute for the item. It is very important that all item balloons in a drawing are the same size. If you use an item balloon block and scale it to a larger/smaller size, make sure all item balloons used have the same scale.

Creating an Item Balloon Block

Switch to layer 0.
Draw a circle with diameter of 0.5.

Define an item attribute as shown in the dialog box. The insertion point should be the center of the circle.

TIP: Create your blocks on layer 0. If you do this, they will adopt the characters of the layer where they are inserted.

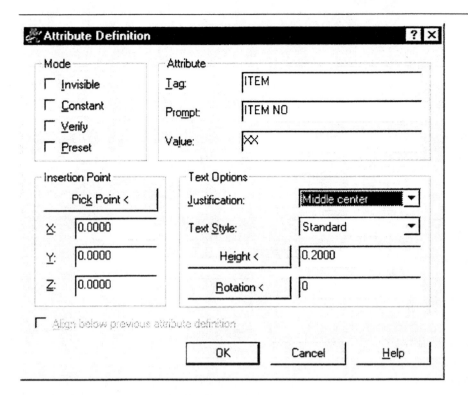

Note the Justification is set to Middle Center.
This will automatically align the text to the center of the balloon.

I have assumed that we will be creating assemblies of less than 100 parts. For more than two digits, we would have to make the circle larger.

Use Make Block to create a local block of the item balloon.

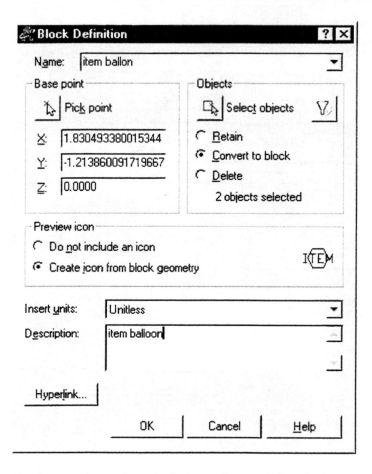

For the base point, select the left quadrant of the circle.

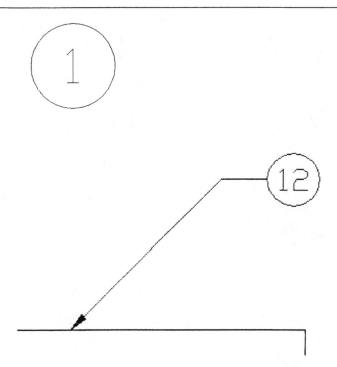

Notice how the text stays centered nicely regardless of whether it is one or two digits.

Creating a Parts List Block

Most companies have two different parts list blocks: one block for the header and one block for the item.

Use your title block to help you set up your parts list blocks. Open your custom title block drawing.

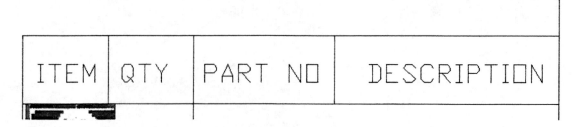

First we create the parts list header. Set ORTHO ON. Use DTEXT to create the word ITEM. Then use COPY MULTIPLE to copy the item text four times. Use DDEDIT to modify the text values to QTY, PART NO, and DESCRIPTION.

By setting ORTHO ON and using COPY MULTIPLE or ARRAY, you keep the text items on the same line.

Use BMAKE to define the header as a block.

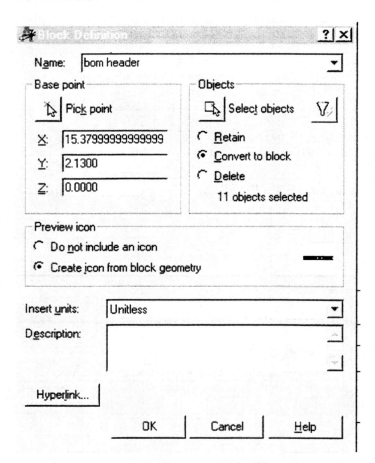

For the base point, select the lower right corner of the block.

Copy the header block and explode it.

Use the text insertion point to help line up your attributes.

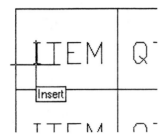

You can place a point and then erase the text or define the attributes using the text insertion points and then erase the dtext items.

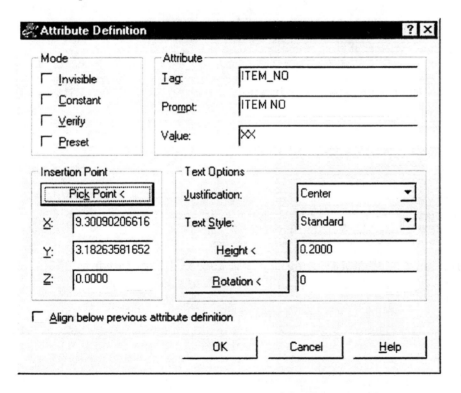

Set the Justification for the Item No and the Quantity as Center.
Set the Justification for the Part No and Description as Left.

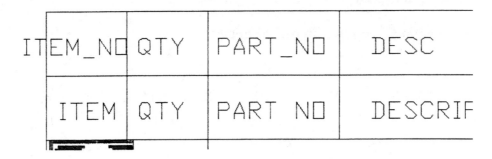

Block your item list.

Use the lower left corner as your insertion point.

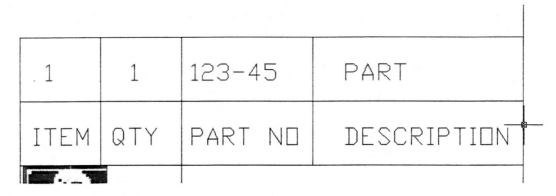

The blocks we just created are shown here.

Using an EXCEL SPREADSHEET

Another way to add a parts list into a drawing is to use an EXCEL spreadsheet. Many drafters like this method as they find it faster and easier to edit a parts list.

1			
2			
3			
4			
5	4	1	123-89	PIN
6	3	1	123-57	KNOB
7	2	1	123-56	LINK
8	1	1	123-45	BODY
9	ITEM	QTY	PART NUMBER	DESCRIPTION
10			
11			
12			

Create your parts list in EXCEL as shown.
Add a border or you will not see lines around the text.

Highlight only the cells you wish to paste into your drawing.

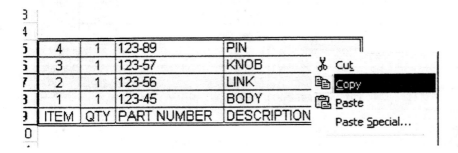

Right click and select 'Copy'.

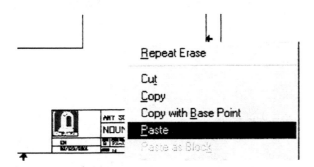

Switch to your AutoCAD drawing.
Right click and select 'Paste'.

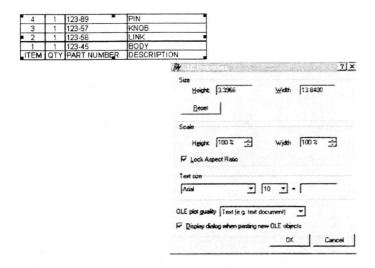

You will see the selected cells and a dialog box. Press 'OK'.

4	1	123-89	PIN
3	1	123-57	KNOB
2	1	123-56	LINK
1	1	123-45	BODY
ITEM	QTY	PART NUMBER	DESCRIPTION

	ANY SCHOOL		
	NOUN, ADJECTIVE		

EM	SIZE B	FSCM NO. PX-X	DWG NO. PX -X	REV A
08/23/2001	SCALE 1:1		SHEET 1 OF 1	

Move and scale the spreadsheet into the correct location.

Creating an Assembly using XREFs

External references are an excellent tool to create an assembly drawing. This requires a certain amount of pre-planning when creating your detail drawings. All the isometric or front views in your detail drawings should be oriented in a way that would work with an assembly drawing.

Start a new file to be used for an assembly drawing.

Use the XREF Manager to locate the drawings to be used for the assembly drawing.

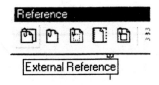

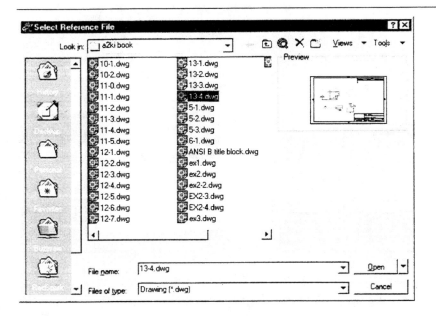

Locate the detail drawings to be used.

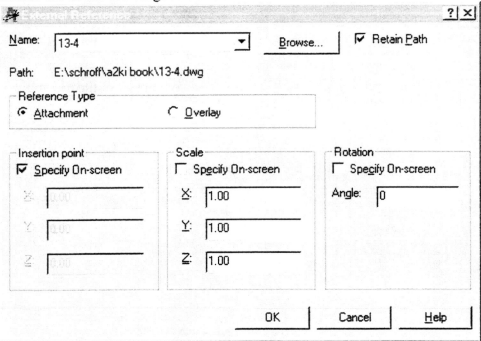

Specify the Reference Type as an Attachment.

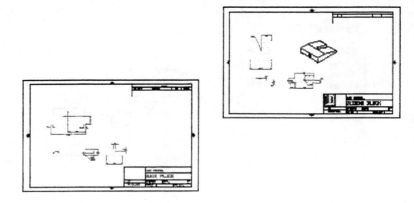

Load all the detail drawings to be used for the assembly into the drawing.

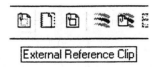

Use XCLIP to select only the isometric view or front view to be used in the assembly drawing.

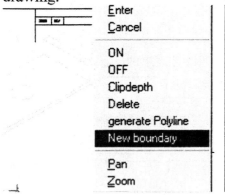

Select the external reference. Then right click and select 'New boundary'.

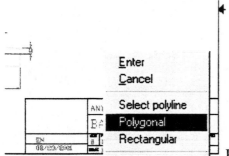 Right click and select 'Polygonal' to create an irregular clipping of the desired view.

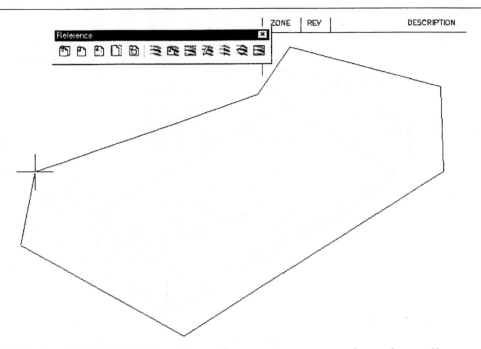

Using the POLYGONAL option allows us to create an irregular outline around the desired view.

TIP: Turning OFF OSNAP will prevent you from creating a bad XCLIP.

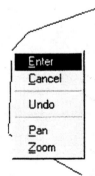

When you are done specifying the boundary, right click and select ENTER.

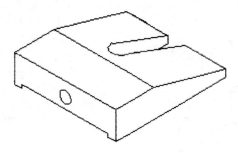

Once you are done with the XCLIP, you can move the XREFs using the MOVE tool to get them into position.

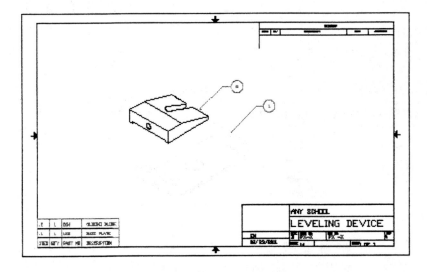

Add item balloons, parts list, title block and general notes, if needed.

Assembly Project #1

Create a detail drawing for each part
Create an isometric view of the following assembly.
Place item balloons for each part.
Create a parts list using the proper format.
Use proper annotation for all fasteners.

Arrange the parts so it is clear how the parts fit together.

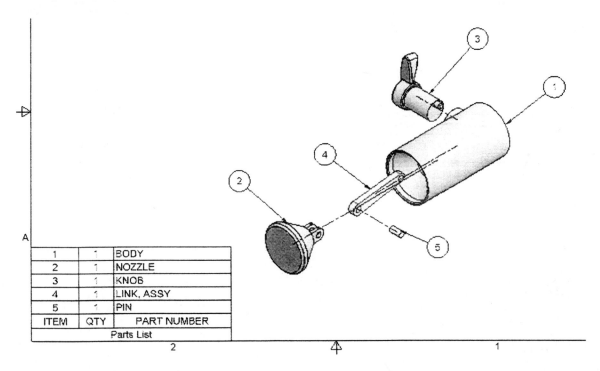

ITEM	QTY	PART NUMBER
1	1	BODY
2	1	NOZZLE
3	1	KNOB
4	1	LINK, ASSY
5	1	PIN

Parts List

PART 1:

BODY

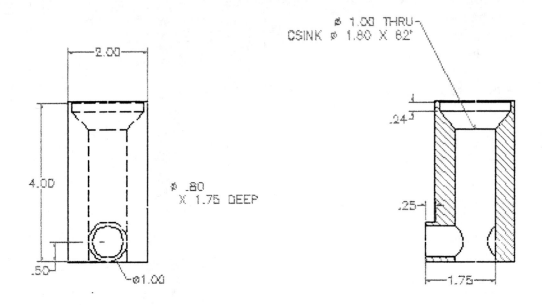

PART 2

LINK

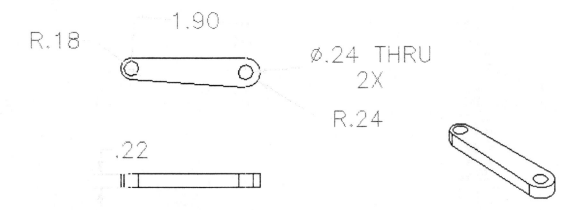

Part 3

Knob

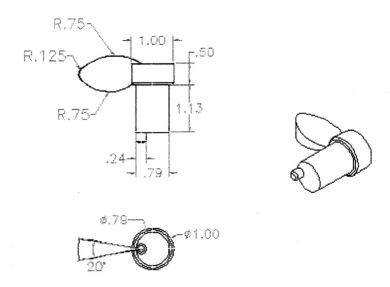

Chamfer .03 x 45 TYP.

PART 4

NOZZLE

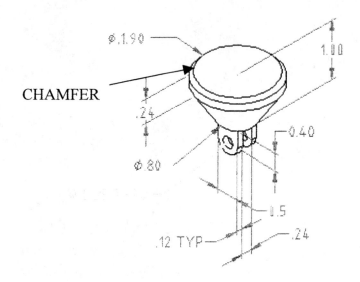

CHAMFER .08 X 45 DEGREES

PART 5

PIN

0.25 DIAMETER X 0.48 LONG
CHAMFER BOTH ENDS .03 X 45 DEGREES

ASSEMBLY PROJECT #2

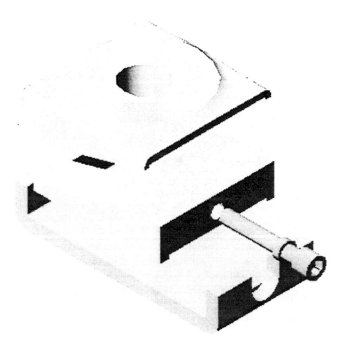

Create a detail drawing for each part
Create an isometric view of the following assembly.
Place item balloons for each part.
Create a parts list using the proper format.
Use proper annotation for all fasteners.

Arrange the parts so it is clear how the parts fit together.

PART 1

BASE PLATE

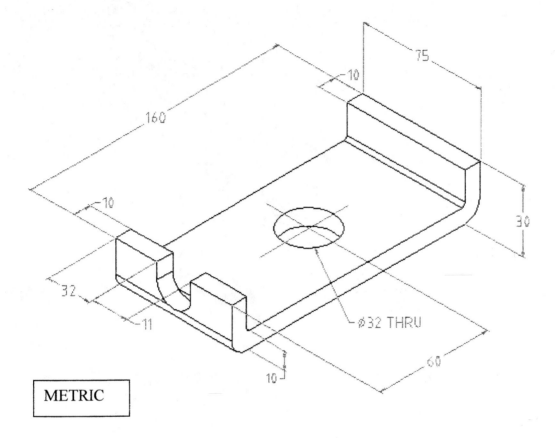

METRIC

PART 2

SLIDING BLOCK

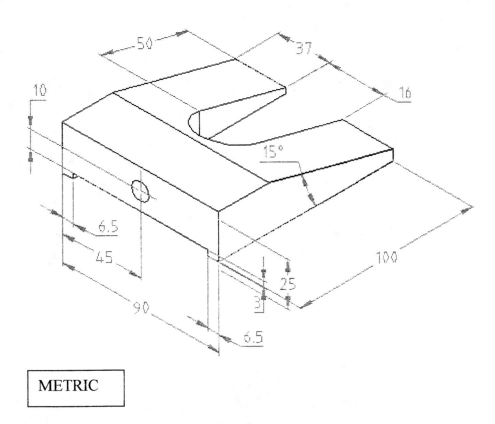

METRIC

PART 3
LIFTING BLOCK

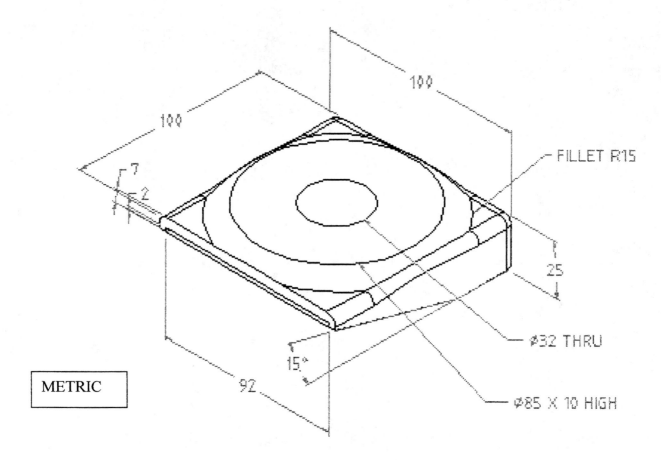

METRIC

FILLET R15

25

Ø32 THRU

Ø85 X 10 HIGH

100

100

7

2

15°

92

ALL FILLETS R5 UNLESS OTHERWISE SPECIFIED

PART 4
ADJUSTING SCREW

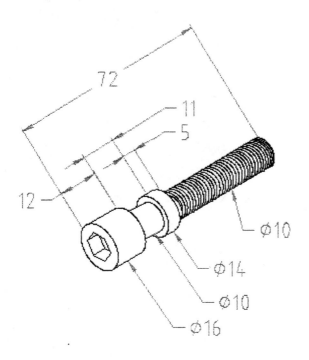

M10-6 X 34 MM L
HEX SOCKET HEAD

METRIC

Notes:

Lesson 14
Reverse Engineering

Most drafters learn how to create drawings from sketches, but in the workplace, you will often be asked to create a drawing from a part. This can occur for several reasons:

- Your company has decided to manufacture a knock-off of a competitor's product

- The drawing for a part is unavailable because it is in an incompatible format for your company's software

- A hard drive crashes with all the drawing file data and the drafter needs to recreate documentation

When confronted with creating a drawing from a part, many drafters get easily frustrated.

Learning Objectives

- Reading a caliper
- Techniques for Reverse Engineering

Take it one step at a time...

- Examine the part carefully

- Take the overall dimensions

- Plan your drawing

In order to determine the dimensions of a part, whether to verify a part for part inspection or to reverse engineer a part, the drafter will use a caliper.

What is a caliper?

A precise measuring device used in mechanical drafting.

Measures both in inches and in millimeters.

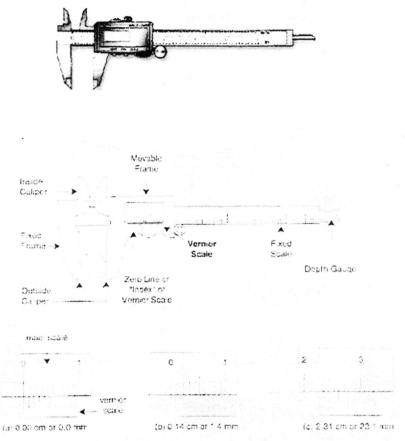

Figure 2. A vernier caliper with various readings

Notice that the cm/mm scale is read by the location of the zero mark on the vernier scale, not the edge of the movable frame. The second reading, in 1/20 mm, is taken by "lining up" a mark on the vernier scale with one of the main scale.

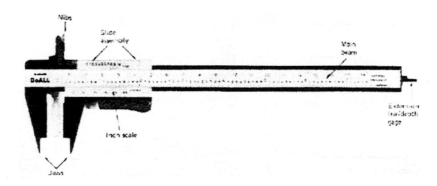

To read a vernier caliper:

Read the large number division first.
Read the small number division.
Read the number of smaller subdivisions. Each represents
0.025 inches to be added to the measurement.
Read which line on the vernier lines up with a line on the
main beam. For each line a thousandth must be added to
the measurement.

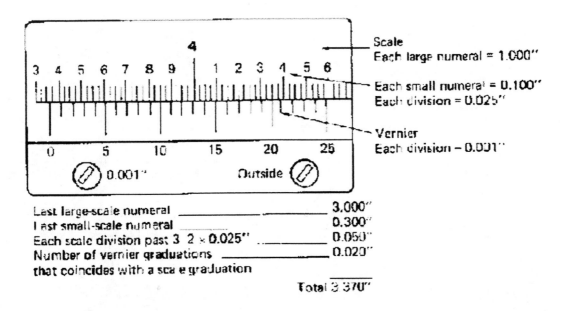

Last large-scale numeral	3.000"
Last small-scale numeral	0.300"
Each scale division past 3 2 × 0.025"	0.050"
Number of vernier graduations	0.020"
that coincides with a scale graduation	
Total	3.370"

Examples of Reading a Caliper

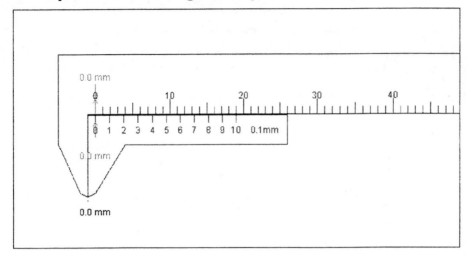

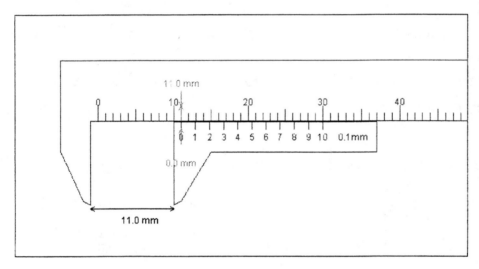

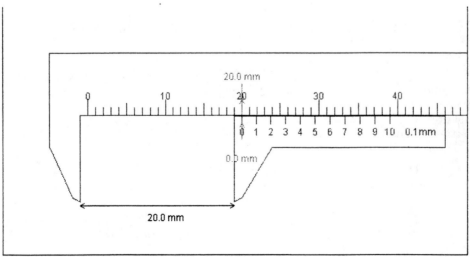

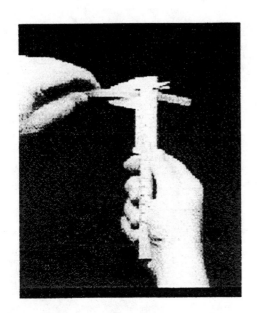

To take measurement:

Place the edge you want to measure between the jaws.

Look for where the 0 lines

up and note the measurement.

Make sure you keep caliper so that it is perpendicular/straight from the position being measured. A common error is to angle the caliper while measuring and this will give the drafter the wrong value. Measure each feature 2-3 times to verify that you are getting the correct value.

Exercise 1:

Have the instructor provide a model for the student to use to practice reverse engineering. The part should require the use of the depth gage, inside and outside caliper.

Exercise 2:

Have the student create an assembly drawing of a small assembly such as a hinge, doorbell, or latch using reverse engineering methodology.

Lesson 15
Document Control

Learning Objectives

- Engineering Changes
- Correcting a redlined drawing

Most drafters don't start out creating drawings from scratch. Your first job in the drafting field will probably be in a department known as Document Control. In this department, drafters correct or edit drawings that have been created by someone else. Document changes can include modifying drawings to update them to current CAD standards, changing existing detail drawings to reflect design changes, or modifying assembly drawings to indicate bill of material changes.

Understanding how to correct a drawing you didn't create and proper document control procedures will help you perform better on the job.

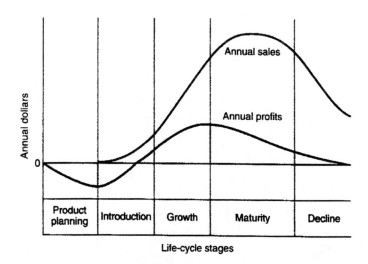

Most products go through the life cycle shown in the above graph. A product goes through the most engineering drafting changes during Product Planning, Introduction, and Growth. During Maturity, a product is usually controlled by a department called Sustaining Engineering. This department deals with issues that occur when the product is out in the field.

Engineering Change Process

ECN - Engineering Change Notice

ECO - Engineering Change Order

ECR - Engineering Change Request

CCB - Change Control Board

The CCB meets to review ECRs and decide what changes are required to improve the product, reduce costs, improve quality, or to resolve vendor issues. If the ECR is approved, an ECO/ECN is issued.

Each company has it's own CCB. Usually, representatives from Engineering, Operations, Purchasing/Finance, and Sales/Marketing sit on the CCB. Each of these departments has an interest in how engineering changes occur.

Once an engineering change is approved, an ECO form is filled out, signed off and submitted to Document Control. This is where the drafter enters the picture.

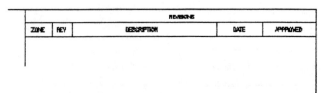

REVISIONS				
ZONE	REV	DESCRIPTION	DATE	APPROVED

In the upper right corner of the title block, you may have noticed this section. This section is called the Revision Block. This section is used to control changes to a drawing.

REVISIONS					
ZONE	REV	DESCRIPTION		DATE	APPROVED

ZONE	Indicates the area where the drafting change occurs. Your title block establishes a grid for your drawing
REV	Indicates the revision level that the drawing was assigned with the change
DESCRIPTION	Describes the engineering change
DATE	Date of engineering change
APPROVED	Usually signed off by the head of Document Control or Engineering

Proper Terms to describe changes

- ADDED
- REVISED
- DELETED

ADDED – Used when a new feature/dimension is added to a drawing

REVISIONS					
ZONE	REV	DESCRIPTION		DATE	APPROVED
A1	B	ADDED .160 THRU .250 CBORE .125 DP		2/23/2001	

REVISED – Says what was changed, always say what it WAS, and what it IS

REVISIONS				
ZONE	REV	DESCRIPTION	DATE	APPROVED
A1	B	ADDED .160 THRU .250 CBORE .125 DP	2/23/2001	
B2	C	REVISED DIM: WAS: 3.50 IS: 2.50	3/23/2001	

DELETED – Say what was removed. You do not need to say WHY it was deleted. This is covered in the engineering change documentation.

REVISIONS				
ZONE	REV	DESCRIPTION	DATE	APPROVED
A1	B	ADDED .160 THRU .250 CBORE .125 DP	2/23/2001	
B2	C	REVISED DIM: WAS: 3.50 IS: 2.50	3/23/2001	
C4	D	DELETED: .25 THK FLANGE	4/15/2001	

Corrections to a drawing to correct typos, incorrect layers or linetypes or other formatting errors are not included in the title block. Only changes that affect FORM, FIT or FUNCTION of a part or assembly are ever documented in the revision block.

FORM –

Changes that affect the shape or size of the part. Changes in material or finish are also considered a FORM change.

FIT –

Changes that affect the tolerance of the part or how it fits with another part.

FUNCTION –

Changes that affect how the part works or is used. For example, changing from a 120V power supply to a 240V power supply. The power supply may have the exact same size and shape as the previous power supply used.

Exercise 1:
Engineering Change

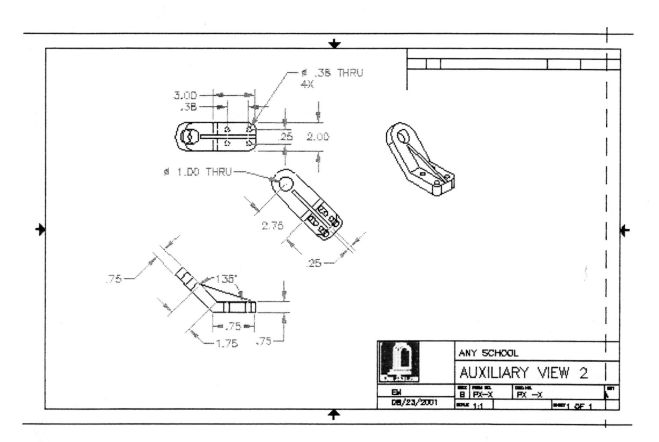

ECO:
REVISE FOUR SMALL HOLES
WAS: 0.38 THRU
IS: 6-32 CSK X 62 DEGREES THRU

Notes:

Lesson 16
Introduction to Customization

Learning Objectives

- Creating Custom Toolbars
- Creating Custom Tools
- Creating a basic Visual Lisp routine

At some point, most drafters decide that they are tired of cluttering up their drawing area with toolbars and seek to consolidate their tools into one single toolbar using only those tools they use most often.

If you right click on any toolbar, you can access 'Customize'.

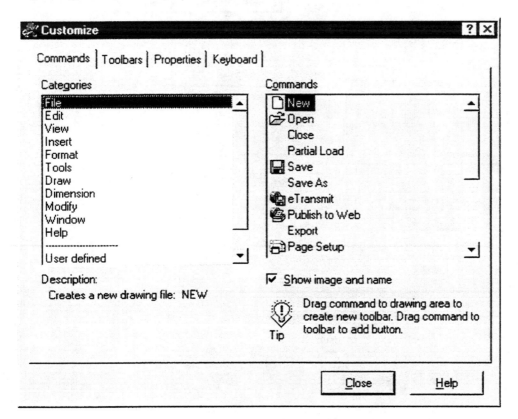

The Customize dialog box appears.

Select the Toolbars tab.

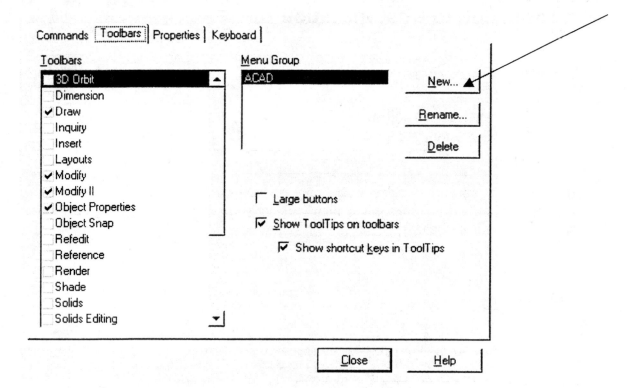

Select the 'New' button.

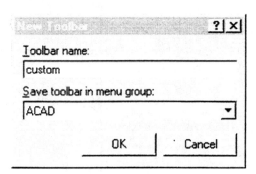

Press 'OK'.

TIP: It is a good idea to create a separate menu group to store custom toolbars. That way you can back up any customization you do. Otherwise, make sure to back up your acad.mnu, acad.mnc, and acad.mns files on a regular basis to an area away from the AutoCAD directory. Then, if you have to reinstall AutoCAD, copy your backup files to restore your custom toolbars and menus. If you create any custom bmps for your toolbars, you should save those in a backup directory as well. If you don't, you will see smiley faces instead of your bitmaps when you restore your custom toolbar.

An empty toolbar will appear in your graphics area.

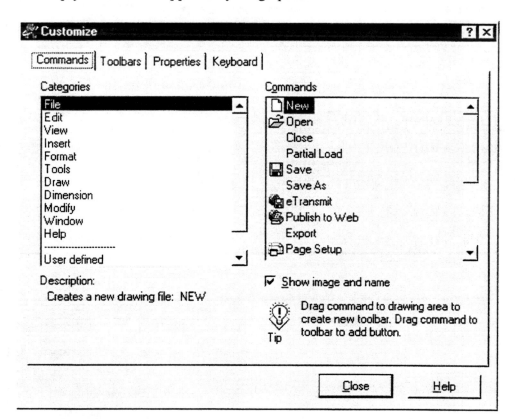

Select the Commands tab.

Drag and drop the tools that you use most often into your toolbar.

If you select a tool by mistake you can delete it by just dragging and dropping it back into the Customization dialog box.

To move icons around on your tool bar, just drag them into the new location.

Now instead of three or four toolbars, you can have just one toolbar with all the tools you need.

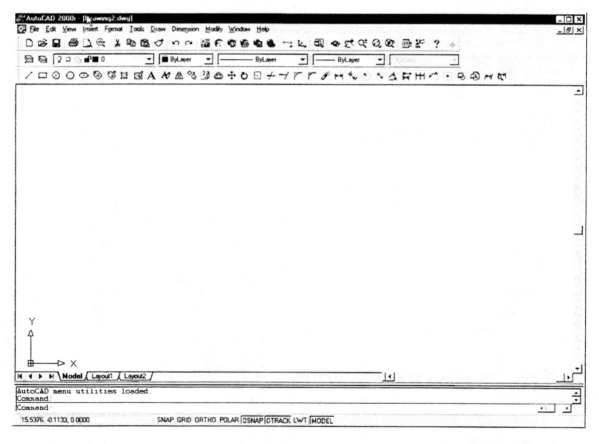

Look how much more space we now have to work in.

Creating a Custom Button

We just saw that there are many more tools available to us than what we see on the standard toolbars and how to create our own custom toolbar. Now we are going to create our own custom button.

When we were creating isometric figures, one of the commands we used was ELLIPSE, ISO. We will now create a button to allow us to create an isometric ellipse without having to do a lot of typing.

First, we look at the steps required to create an isometric ellipse.

The first thing we notice is we need to be in isometric snap before we even get the isometric option for the ellipse.

The sequence of commands we go through to create an isometric ellipse are as follows:

Snap, S, I, ENTER   sets isometric mode
Snap, OFF, ENTER   turns SNAP to GRID off
EL, I,   starts the ellipse, iso command

Now we are ready to create a custom tool to create an isometric ellipse

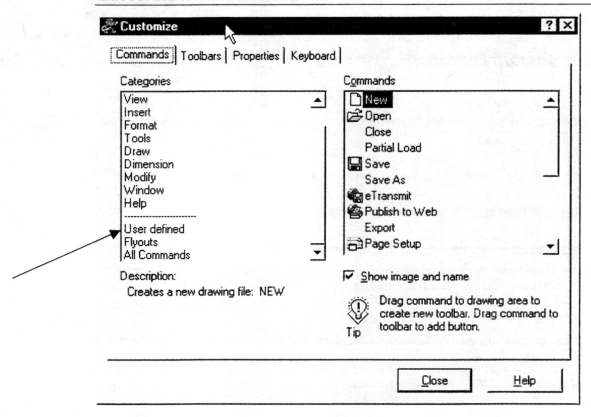

Return to the Customize dialog box. Select the Commands tab.
Highlight the words 'User defined'.

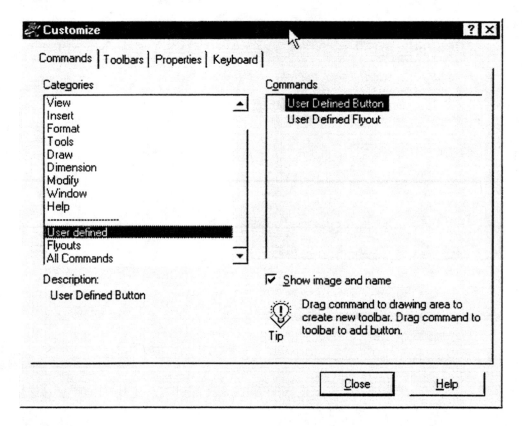

On the right side, you see we can define a User Defined button or a User Defined Flyout. There is a blank button next the words User Defined button. Drag and drop it on to your toolbar.

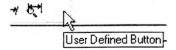

To set the button to perform a custom command, place your mouse over the custom button and right click.

TIP: Do NOT close the Customize Dialog box or you will not be able to edit your button properties.

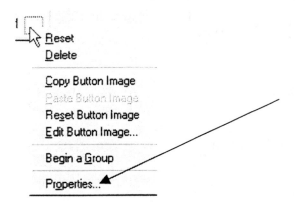

When you right click on the blank button, you will get a menu. Select Properties.

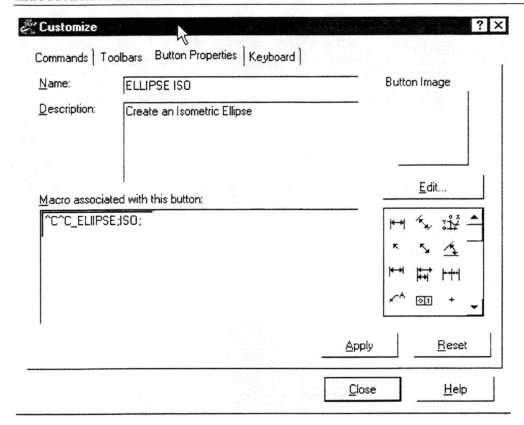

In the Name Field, type ELLIPSE ISO.

In the Description, type Create an Isometric Ellipse (This is the tool tip that will appear when you mouse over the button)

In the Macro area, you will see ^C^C

This cancels out any commands that you may be in the middle of when you select your button.

We then type ELLIPSE;ISO;

Each semi-colon indicates an ENTER.

Next, locate the ellipse icon in the icon window.

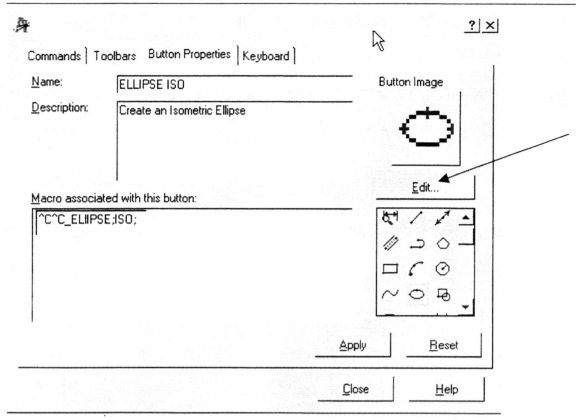

Select the ellipse icon and it will automatically copy over to your button.
Press the Edit button.

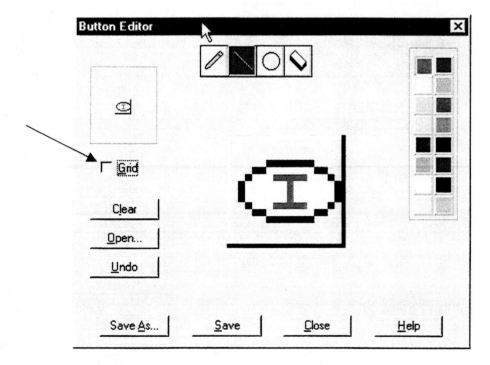

Edit the figure as shown.

You can enable the Grid to make it easier to draw if needed.

Press Save and then Close to save your editing.

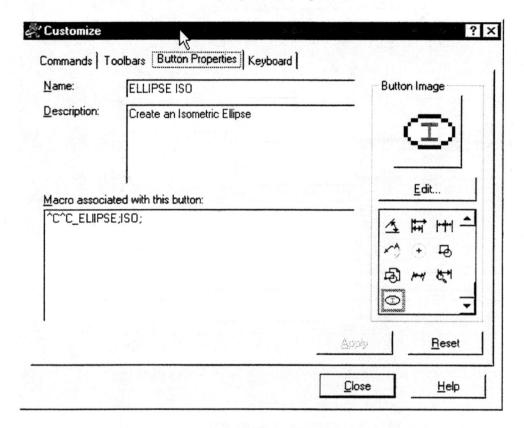

You now see your new icon on the button image. Press 'Apply'.
You will see the image appear on your custom button.

Press 'Close'.

Switch to isometric mode and test your ellipse iso button.

Command: |

Create an Isometric Ellipse

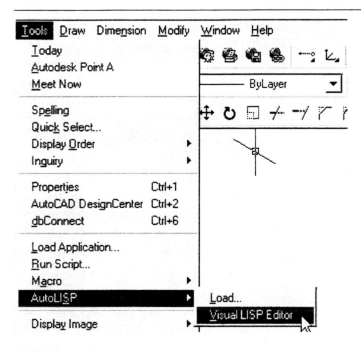

Visual Lisp

Starting in AutoCAD R14, Autodesk included Visual Lisp with AutoCAD. Visual Lisp is a programming language used to create custom routines/macros for use with AutoCAD.

To access the Visual Lisp interface, type 'vlisp' or 'vlide' on the command line. The editor can also be accessed from the menu under Tools->AutoLisp->Visual Lisp Editor.

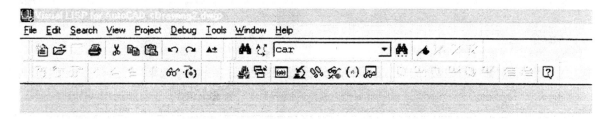

The Visual Lisp interface window appears.

Before we can see all the icons we have to start a new file.

Menu	File->New File
Tool	
Keyboard	Ctrl-N

To create a REMARK or COMMENT, it is preceded by a semi-colon.

```
; THIS IS A COMMENT
```

Visual Lisp automatically color-codes your program to help you in debugging. Comments or remarks are shown in purple. They also are highlighted in gray.

All programs start with a parenthesis and the word DEFUN. DEFUN means Define Function.

```
; THIS IS A COMMENT

(defun
```

Notice that the parenthesis is color-coded red. The word defun is color coded blue to indicate that it is a Visual Lisp command.

We are going to define or create a custom command. To let AutoCAD know that we are defining a command we type c:

```
; THIS IS A COMMENT

(defun c:
```

Next we have to give our command a name. For this example, we'll create a macro to insert our custom title block. We'll call our command itblock.

```
; THIS IS A COMMENT

(defun c:itblock (/)
```

When creating a macro, we look at what commands we use in AutoCAD. We need to suppress all the dialog boxes when inserting a block. The system variable that controls the appearance of dialog boxes is CMDDIA. To turn it off, we set it to 0.

```
; THIS IS A COMMENT

(defun c:itblock (/)
  (command "CMDDIA" 0) ; TURNS DIALOG BOXES OFF
```

The word command is used to initiate an AutoCAD command.

If we want to test if the line works properly, we can highlight it with our mouse and then load it into AutoCAD using the Load Selection tool.

If you switch to the AutoCAD window and look at the command line, you will see that the command was loaded properly.

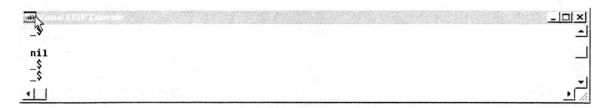

In the Visual Lisp Console, you will see the word nil. This means that the command was loaded properly into AutoCAD and returned a nil value.

Next we need to set the name of the title block to be inserted.

Note down where your block is located including the path. We will then assign that file name and path to a variable.

```
; THIS IS A COMMENT

(defun c:itblock (/)
   (command "CMDDIA" 0) ; TURNS DIALOG BOXES OFF
   (setq bname "e:\\schroff\\a2ki book\\ansi b title block.dwg")
```

We use the Visual Lisp function setq. Setq assigns a variable a value. Bname is the name of the variable. The path and file name is the value assigned to bname. Note that we use two back slashes instead of one to indicate our subdirectories.

Test this line of code by highlighting it and loading it using the Load Selection tool.

```
; THIS IS A COMMENT

(defun c:itblock (/)
   (command "CMDDIA" 0) ; TURNS DIALOG BOXES OFF
   (setq bname "e:\\schroff\\a2ki book\\ansi b title block.dwg")
```

```
_$

"e:\\schroff\\a2ki book\\ansi b title block.dwg"
_$
```

In the Visual Lisp console, we see the value stored in the variable bname.

If we want to keep track of variables and their values, we can use the Watch tool.

Highlight the word bname and select Add Watch

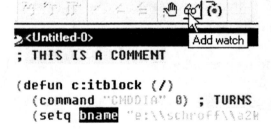

```
; THIS IS A COMMENT

(defun c:itblock (/)
   (command "CMDDIA" 0) ; TURNS
   (setq bname "e:\\schroff\\a2k
```

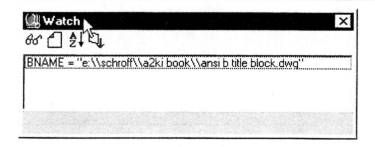

A Watch window will pop up that keeps track of the variables selected.

```
; THIS IS A COMMENT

(defun c:itblock (/)
   (command "CMDDIA" 0) ; TURNS DIALOG BOXES OFF
   (setq bname "ansi b title block.dwg")
   (command "-insert" bname "0,0" "" "" "")
```

TIP: If you are using a template where the title block has already been pre-loaded, you do not have to include the path when designating your title block. This is because the block is already local to the current drawing.

The next line inserts the title block at 0,0. You see three sets of double quotes. A double quote is used to signify an ENTER. When you insert a title block, you are prompted for your X scale, your Y scale, and rotation angle. Each double quote indicates an ENTER to accept the defaults.

itblock.LSP

Load selection

```
; THIS IS A COMMENT

(defun c:itblock (/)
   (command "CMDDIA" 0) ; TURNS DIALOG BOXES OFF
   (setq bname "ansi b title block.dwg"); sets the title block to be used
   (command "-insert" bname "0,0" "" "" "") ; inserts the title block at 0,0
```

Test your code by highlighting it and loading it with the Load Selection tool.

You will then be prompted for all your values for the title block attributes.

Time to finish the routine.

To indicate the end of the function, we close it with a parenthesis.

Many times users will load an AutoLisp routine, but will forget the custom command required to run it.

We add a prompt to tell the user the custom command to run the routine.

```
; THIS IS A COMMENT

(defun c:itblock (/)
   (command "CMDDIA" 0) ; TURNS DIALOG BOXES OFF
   (setq bname "ansi D title block.dwg"); sets the title block to be used
   (command "insert" bname "0,0" "" "" "") ; inserts the title block at 0,0
); end defun

(princ "Type 'itblock' to insert title block. ") ; tell the user what they need to type
```

Note that we use a single quote around 'itblock' and double quotes around the entire text for the prompt.

Save your file as itblock.

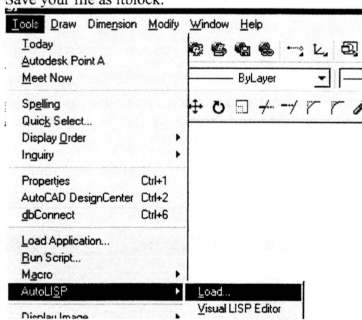

To load an AutoLisp routine, from the menu Tools->AutoLisp->load or type 'appload' at the command line.

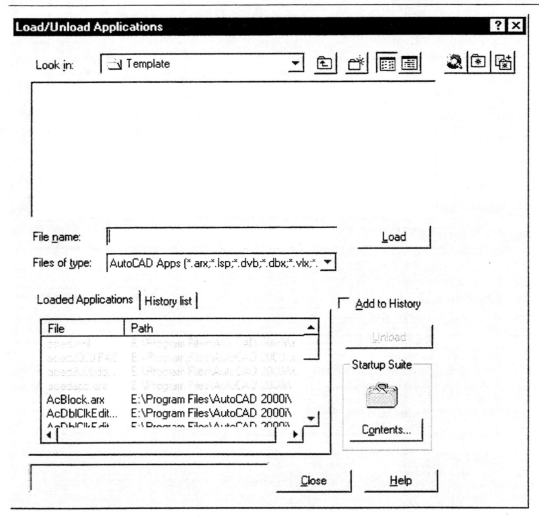

A Load Applications dialog box appears.

Locate the lisp routine we just created.

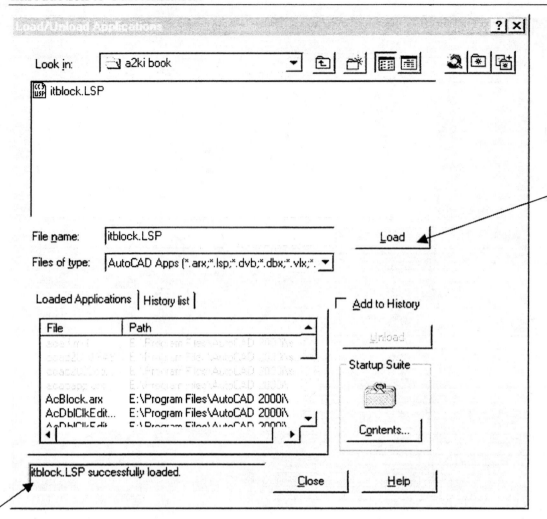

Press the Load button.

If it loaded successfully, you will see a message to that effect as shown.

Press 'Close'.

On the command line in AutoCAD, you will see the prompt you created.

Type 'itblock' and see what happens.

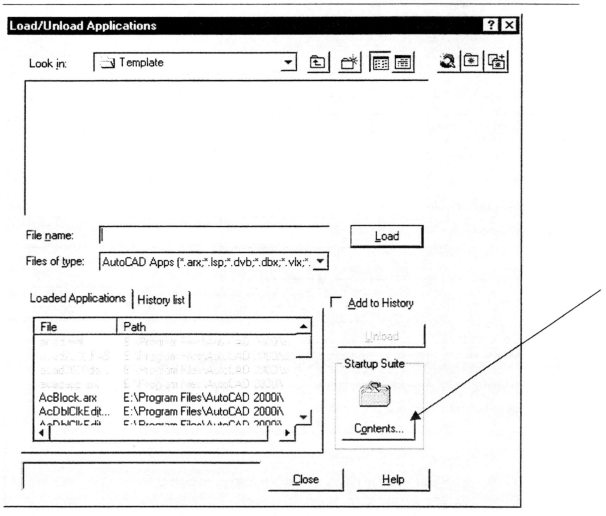

To have our lisp routine automatically load any time we open AutoCAD we can add it to our Startup Suite. Select the Contents button in the Load Applications dialog box.

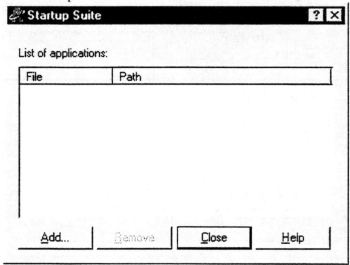

Press the Add button and locate the itblock routine we just created.

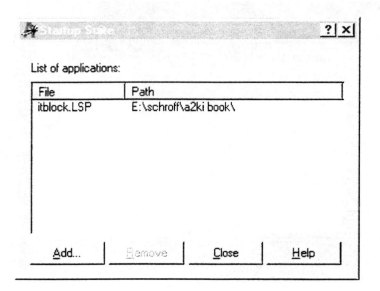

Press 'Close'.

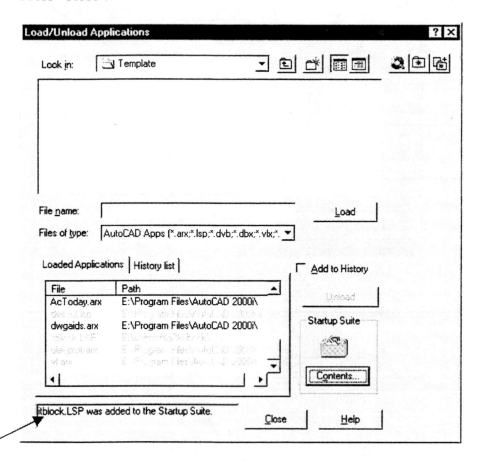

Press 'Close'.

Exercise 1:

Itblock button

Create a custom button to insert a title block using the routine created in Lesson 16

Exercise 2:
Item Balloon

Create an AutoLisp program to insert an item balloon using leader and the item balloon block we created earlier.

Notes:

QUIZ 4

1. You attach a XREF to a drawing, save, and then go out to lunch. A co-worker opens up the drawing being used as a XREF and makes some changes, saves it to the same location, and then goes home early. You return from lunch and re open the drawing you were working on. You see:
    A.   the same XREF you originally inserted - no change
    B.   the updated XREF
    C.   a blank space where the XREF used to be
    D.   nothing...your drawing is now corrupted and can not be opened. Complain to the boss and get your co-worker fired.

2. External references are used instead of inserting a global block because:
    A.   External references keep the size of the file small.
    B.   External references will automatically update whenever the drawing is reopened.
    C.   edits are faster.
    D.   All of the above

3. The icon shown:
    A.   brings up the XREF dialog box
    B.   binds a XREF
    C.   clips a XREF
    D.   turns off the XREF frame

4. The icon shown:
    A.   brings up the XREF Manager dialog box
    B.   initiates XCLIP
    C.   binds a XREF
    D.   initiates XCLIPFRAME

5. The menu header used to load an AutoLISP application is:
    A.   TOOLS
    B.   INSERT
    C.   FORMAT
    D.   FILE

6. Select the correct LISP routine:
    A.   (defun c:ze ()(command "{zoom" "e"))
    B.   (defun c:ze (command "zoom" "e"))
    C.   (defun c:ze ()(command zoom e))
    D.   (defun c:ze ()(command "zoom" "e"))

7. The three different ways to draw a thread are:
    A.   BASIC, INTERMEDIATE, AND ADVANCED
    B.   BASIC, DETAILED, AND COMPLEX
    C.   DETAILED, SCHEMATIC, AND SIMPLIFIED
    D.   SCHEMATIC, SIMPLE, AND BASIC

8. You see the following annotation on a drawing:
.250 -20 UNC-2A
.250 stands for:
    A.   nominal diameter
    B.   number of threads per inch
    C.   thread form
    D.   class of fit

9. Instead of using a global block, you can create a link to an external drawing using an external reference.   (T / F)

10. Layer names for external references use the following format; where PLAN is the file name and WALLS is the layer name:
    A.   PLAN/WALLS
    B.   PLAN0WALLS
    C.   PLAN:WALLS
    D.   PLAN|WALLS

11. The higher the class, the tighter the fit...1 is the tightest.   (T / F)

12. External thread classes are 1B, 2B, 3B, and internal thread classes are 1A, 2A, and 3A.   (T / F)

13. The file extension used on AutoLISP routines is:
     A. dwg
     B. txt
     C. lsp
     D. dwt

14. You can use a drawing as an external reference even if it is in use by another user.   (T / F)

15. Reverse engineering means:
     A. creating a drawing from scratch
     B. drawing everything backwards
     C. creating a drawing using someone else's idea
     D. creating a drawing from a physical object

16. The icon shown
     A. Brings up the XREF Manager Dialog Box
     B. Initiates the XCLIP command
     C. Initiates the XCLIPFRAME command
     D. Attaches an XREF

17. The toolbar shown is:
     A. Reference
     B. XREF
     C. Image
     D. OLE

18.   Calipers cannot be used to measure the inside of holes.   (T / F)

|D|ImportText..|
| |Help|

Modify character properties.   Ln 1 Col 1

Modify character properties.   Ln 1 Col 1

19.   To add hole annotation symbols to your drawing, access symbols here in your MTEXT dialog box.

20.   Calipers can not be used to measure the depth of holes.   (T / F)

21.   You use a special file for starting a new drawing. This special file has various items such as drawing units and limits, layers, dimension styles, already created. In some cases, there may be blocks already inserted. This file has the extension of:
          A.   DWT
          B.   DWG
          C.   DWF
          D.   DWX

22.   When mating parts are shown on an assembly drawing, section lining for both parts are done at the same angle.   (T / F)

23.   The three methods for assembling parts are:
          A.   SCREWS, BOLTS, AND NAILS
          B.   WELDING, ADHESIVES, AND FASTENERS
          C.   GLUE, SPIT, AND HAIRSPRAY
          D.   GREASE, GRIME, AND GRIT

24.	The command to load an AutoLisp routine into AutoCAD is:
        A.	LOAD
        B.	APPLOAD
        C.	LISPLOAD
        D.	ALOAD

25.	90% of all commercial and industrial fasteners are 1A and 1B.　　　　(T / F)

ANSWERS:

1) B;2) D; 3) A; 4) B; 5) A; 6) B; 7) C; 8) A; 9) T; 10) D; 11) F; 12) F; 13) C; 14) T;
15) D; 16) C; 17) A; 18) F; 19) B; 20) F; 21) A; 22) F; 23) B; 24) B; 25) F

Index